ABOUT THE AUTHOR

Edward Callan teaches English at Western Michigan University, where he also assists with the African Studies program. He has lived in South Africa, having received his B.A. from Witwatersrand University and his doctorate from the University of South Africa. He has done post-doctoral work in African Studies at Oxford University.

His essays on contemporary literature have appeared in various journals, including *Twentieth Century Literature, The Southern Review, The Christian Scholar, Renascense,* and the *University of Toronto Quarterly.* He has reviewed for *Saturday Review, New York Times Book Review, Choice,* and *The Critic.* He has contributed to *Encyclopedia Americana* and the *New International Yearbook,* and has collaborated with Alan Paton in preparing THE LONG VIEW for publication in the United States.

TWAYNE'S WORLD AUTHORS SERIES

A Survey of the World's Literature

Sylvia E. Bowman, Indiana University

GENERAL EDITOR

SOUTH AFRICA

Joseph Jones, University of Texas

EDITOR

Alan Paton

(*TWAS 40*)

TWAYNE'S WORLD AUTHORS SERIES (TWAS)

*The purpose of TWAS is to survey the major writers
—novelists, dramatists, historians, poets, philosophers,
and critics—of the nations of the world. Among the
national literatures covered are those of Australia,
Canada, China, Eastern Europe, France, Germany,
Greece, India, Italy, Japan, Latin America, New Zea-
land, Poland, Russia, Scandinavia, Spain, and the
African nations, as well as Hebrew, Yiddish, and
Latin Classical literatures. This survey is comple-
mented by Twayne's United States Authors Series
and English Authors Series.*

*The intent of each volume in these series is to present
a critical-analytical study of the works of the writer;
to include biographical and historical material that
may be necessary for understanding, appreciation,
and critical appraisal of the writer; and to present all
material in clear, concise English—but not to vitiate
the scholarly content of the work by doing so.*

Alan Paton

By EDWARD CALLAN
Western Michigan University

Twayne Publishers, Inc. :: New York

To Claire

To Claire

Preface

Since his first novel, *Cry, the Beloved Country*, appeared in 1948, Alan Paton has been accepted as one of the foremost interpreters of South African life and society through the medium of literature. Prior to 1948 he had gained a fine professional reputation for his creative approach to problems of penal reform; and in more recent years he has felt compelled to enter public life as an active leader of the Liberal Party to promote the spirit of non-racial democracy in South Africa. The principal aim of this book has been to describe and evaluate Alan Paton's literary achievement in fiction, drama, biography, and poetry. But I have also sought, where possible, to show the related significance of his writings on sociology, politics, and religion, and of his practical endeavors in creative social welfare as well as in the work of the South African Liberal Party which he has led as National President since 1958.

To provide a reasonably rounded view of Alan Paton's achievements, I have devoted two chapters to his work and writings prior to the appearance of *Cry, the Beloved Country*. The first of these combines an assessment of his early creative writing with an account of the social and political environment in South Africa during his formative years. A second chapter deals with his work at Diepkloof Reformatory, his writings on penal reform, and the evolution of his non-racial outlook. Subsequent chapters treat his novels, short fiction, drama, poetry, and biography chiefly in the sequence of their publication. The closing chapter includes brief descriptions of his books and pamphlets on political, philosophical, and religious questions. In general, it has not seemed possible, or desirable, to separate Alan Paton the literary artist from the creative social reformer and man of affairs whose humanitarian spirit is deeply rooted in Christian principles.

The writer of any book dealing, even indirectly, with racially classified South African society encounters thorny problems of

7

terminology. It may, therefore, be useful to remind the American reader, in particular, that the term *South Africa* when used in this book refers only to the present Republic of South Africa occupying the southern tip of the African continent between Rhodesia and the Cape of Good Hope, and not to all of Africa south of the Sahara. In keeping with its policy of rigid racial separation known as *apartheid*, the Republic of South Africa officially classifies its population into four groups. In this system of classification the term *European* is used to describe the group that includes all white people. This white group which rules the state consists of two language groups, namely, those who speak English and those who speak the South African form of Dutch now known as *Afrikaans*. The English-speaking white people usually refer to themselves as *South Africans;* the Afrikaans-speaking white people, who were once termed *South African Dutch*, or *Boers*, now prefer to refer to themselves as *Afrikaners*. The term *Afrikaner* refers, therefore, to the majority group among the white minority, and not to the descendants of the African tribes indigenous to the continent.

The largest population group in South Africa is composed of indigenous African people. Members of this group, now classified as *Bantu*, and once classified as *Native*, prefer to refer to themselves as *Africans*. In this book the term *African* is used except where references to official documents and departments necessarily retain the form in the original, e.g., *The Bantu Education Act*, or the *Department of Native Affairs*.

There are two smaller population groups in South Africa officially classified as *Asiatics* and *Colored*. Since the first group is comprised chiefly of people of Indian origin, the term *Indian* is used in this book. The term *Colored* in South African race classification is not a synonym for *Negro* or *dark-skinned*, since it excludes both Africans and Indians. It includes all people of mixed racial ancestry. A significant group of people classified as *Colored* have Malayan ancestry and were formerly known as *Cape Malays* or *Cape Colored People*. When necessary for distinction I use the latter term.

The term *non-racial* as used in this book is derived from Alan Paton's writings on race relations and the program of the Liberal Party. It implies, among other things, that this system of rigidly classifying people in racial groups should be abandoned in favor of some common description for all inhabitants of South Africa.

The arrangement of the bibliography of Alan Paton's writings at the conclusion of the text corresponds, approximately, to the order of the chapters. Page numbers in parentheses included in the text refer to the U.S. standard edition of the work under discussion. Variant titles are indicated as follows: D. indicates *Debbie Go Home* and T., *Tales from a Troubled Land;* H. indicates *Hofmeyr*, and S.A.T., *South African Tragedy.*

EDWARD CALLAN

Western Michigan University

Acknowledgments

I acknowledge a special debt of gratitude to Alan Paton for graciously and patiently responding to my questions, for permitting me to quote from his published writings, including his early poems, and for agreeing to check the Chronology for accuracy. I also acknowledge a special debt to Miss Ruth Shirley Lundie, of the University of Natal Library, who so willingly supplied me with copies of Mr. Paton's undergraduate writings in the *Natal University College Magazine* and other materials not otherwise obtainable. I am also indebted to Dr. Quintin Whyte, Director of the South African Institute of Race Relations, for materials from the Institute library, and to the library staffs of Smith College and Western Michigan University for assisting me in locating materials. I am grateful to Miss Janice Davis, Miss Julie Watson, and Mr. Barry Donath for reading the manuscript and suggesting improvements.

I wish to make special acknowledgment for permission to quote from the following works still in copyright:

To Charles Scribner's Sons for permission to quote from *Cry, the Beloved Country, Too Late the Phalarope, Tales from a Troubled Land,* and *South African Tragedy: The Life and Times of Jan Hofmeyr,* by Alan Paton, and *Sponono,* a play by Alan Paton and Krishna Shah.

To Frederick A. Praeger, Inc. for permission to quote from *Hope for South Africa.*

To Crown Publishers, Inc. for permission to quote from the introduction to *Quartet: New Voices from South Africa,* edited by Richard Rive. Copyright 1963 by Crown Publishers, Inc.

To the Editors of *Contact* (Cape Town, South Africa) for permission to quote from Alan Paton's Series, *The Long View.*

To the Editors of *Contrast* (South African Literary Journal Ltd.) for permission to quote from "A Deep Experience" (De-

11

cember, 1961), "The Hofmeyr Biography" (October, 1964), and "I Have Approached a Moment of Sterility" (November, 1961).

To Mr. Studs Terkel for permission to quote from "Four Interviews in South Africa: Alan Paton," in the May, 1963, issue of *Perspective on Ideas and the Arts.*

To Dr. Quintin Whyte, Director of the South African Institute of Race Relations, for permission to quote from the Institute's publications, "The Prevention of Crime," in *Race Relations,* XII (1945); *The Non-European Offender* (1945); *Community and Crime* (1948); and *Freedom as a Reformatory Instrument* (1948).

Contents

Contents

Chronology

1903   January 11, Alan Stewart Paton born at Pietermaritzburg, then Administrative Capital of the British Colony of Natal; father, James Paton, a civil servant, born in Scotland; mother, Eunice, Natal-born and a former teacher.

1910   Union of South Africa formed, incorporating the two former British Colonies, Natal and Cape of Good Hope, and the two former Boer republics, Transvaal and Orange Free State.

1915–   Attended Maritzburg College, a high school, not a univer-
1918   sity, at which he later taught.

1919–   Attended Natal University College (now the University of
1924   Natal); published poetry, short drama, and fiction in *Natal University College Magazine*. Active in student affairs, Dramatic Society, and Students' Christian Association.

1920   Sonnet "To a Picture" in *Natal University College Magazine*.

1921   Poems "The Sea" and "Ladysmith (Midnight on the Battlefields)" in *Natal University College Magazine*.

1922   Graduated, B.Sc. degree, with distinction in Physics; three sonnets, ballad "Song of the Northward-Bound," prose "On Boots," verse drama in three short acts "His Excellency the Governor" in *Natal University College Magazine*.

1923   Poems including "Old Til," in *Natal University College Magazine*.

1924   Two sonnets, poem "Gemellia," and dramatic monologue "Felip'" in *Natal University College Magazine;* awarded Higher Education Diploma (qualification for high school teaching); sent to England by the students of Natal University College as their representative to the first Imperial Conference of Students. Toured England and Scotland by motorcycle.

1925– Taught mathematics at Ixopo High School for white chil-
1928 dren.

1926 With Cyril Armitage and Reg Pearse, founded the Students' Christian Association annual boys camp in Natal.

1927 Friendship with Jan H. Hofmeyr begun at Students' Christian Association camp at Umgababa.

1928 July 2, married Doris Olive Francis, in St. John's Anglican
Church, Ixopo.

1928– Taught at Maritzburg College. Wrote, and destroyed, two
1934 or three novels of Natal country life.

1930 David Paton born.

1934 Poem "The New Physics" in *Natal University College Magazine*. Completed the examinations, but not the thesis, for
the M.Ed. degree, University of South Africa, and was
later awarded the B.Ed. degree, with distinction, in respect of his success in these examinations. Seriously ill
with enteric fever.

1935– Principal of Diepkloof Reformatory, Johannesburg, for Af-
1946 rican boys. Wrote on education and penal reform for various journals.

1936 Jonathan Paton born; "Jan Hendrik Hofmeyr—An Appreciation," in *South African Opinion* (September 18).

1938 Centenary celebrations of the Great Trek; grew a beard
and went to the Voortrekker Centenary Celebrations at
Pretoria in an ox-wagon flying the Vierkleur (flag of the
Transvaal Republic).

1939 Volunteered for military duty in World War II; not eligi-
ble on grounds of essential occupation; became Chairman
of combined Y.M.C.A. and Toc-H (Talbot House) War
Services.

1940 December 16, Athol Paton, Alan's brother, killed in the
battle of El Wak, first engagement of the South African
forces in the Abyssinian and Somaliland campaigns of
World War II.

1943– Series of articles on crime, punishment, and penal reform
1944 commissioned by *The Forum*.

1944 "The Treatment of Non-European Crime," an address to
the National Social Welfare Conference, 1944, published
as *The Non-European Offender;* "Educational Needs of

the Adolescent," in two parts, *Transvaal Education News,* September and October.

1945 "The Prevention of Crime," address to the National Conference organized jointly by the South African Institute of Race Relations and the Social Services Association of South Africa, published in *Race Relations: Special Crime Number.*

1946 Took leave of absence to study penal and correctional institutions in Europe, the United States, and Canada. Attended a Conference of Christians and Jews at Oxford as Chairman of one of its committees; began *Cry, the Beloved Country* in Trondheim, Norway.

1948 *Freedom as a Reformatory Instrument,* an account of reform systems in Europe and America; "Juvenile Delinquency and its Treatment," an address to a National Conference organized by the Penal Reform League; February 2, *Cry, the Beloved Country* published in New York, later in Britain and South Africa; May 26, victory of Dr. D. F. Malan's Nationalist Party over United Party, led by General Smuts and Jan Hofmeyr, introduced policy of *apartheid;* Paton resigned from Diepkloof Reformatory to devote his time to writing; December 3, Jan Hofmeyr died.

1949 Received Ainsfield-Wolf Award (U.S.) and London *Times* Special Book Award for *Cry, the Beloved Country;* visited United States for Broadway opening of *Lost in the Stars;* began work on the biography of Jan Hofmeyr.

1950 Filming of *Cry, the Beloved Country* commenced; Alexander Korda director.

1951 *South Africa Today; Christian Unity: A South African View* (3rd Peter Ainslie Memorial Lecture); *Cry, the Beloved Country* serialized in *Drum* (Johannesburg); first of the Diepkloof short stories, "Worst Thing in His Life," in *Trek* (S.A.).

1952 Wrote *Salute to My Greatgrandchildren;* decided to put aside work on the biography *Hofmeyr* and proceed no further during Mrs. Hofmeyr's lifetime since she began to dislike the idea of a biography that was not to be simply a record of her son's public life; individual poems and short stories published.

1953 *Too Late the Phalarope* (New York and London); Liberal
      Party formed; with his wife, worked at tuberculosis settle-
      ment for non-whites in Natal.
1954 Toured United States to write on race relations for *Col-
      liers;* Hon.L.H.D., Yale; addressed World Council of
      Churches' meetings, Evanston, Illinois; *Cry, the Beloved
      Country: A Verse Drama,* adapted by Felicia Komai, pre-
      sented in the church of St. Martin-in-the-Fields, London.
1955 *The Land and People of South Africa* (New York and Lon-
      don), for high school students in United States and Britain.
1956 *South Africa in Transition* with Dan Weiner (New York
      and London); elected Chairman of the South African Lib-
      eral Party; became trustee of Treason Trial Defence Fund
      (later broadened into Defence and Aid Fund); accom-
      panied archaeological expedition seeking a lost city in the
      Aha Mountains, Kalahari desert; dramatized version of
      Too Late the Phalarope by Robert Yale Libott presented
      at the Belasco Theater, New York.
1958 *Hope for South Africa; The People Wept;* helped to inau-
      gurate *Contact,* a liberal fortnightly; National President of
      the Liberal Party; attended All African Church Confer-
      ence in Nigeria; began his series "The Long View" in
      Contact; visited the Belgian Congo in July-August; Diep-
      kloof Reformatory closed down; Dr. Verwoerd new Prime
      Minister.
1959 Delivered Stafford Cripps Memorial Sermon in St. Paul's
      Cathedral, London; published as *The Christian Approach
      to Racial Problems in the Modern World; The Last Jour-
      ney,* a play about Dr. Livingstone, first produced in Lu-
      saka, N. Rhodesia; four poems in Guy Butler (ed.), *A
      Book of South African Verse;* poem, *Meditation for a
      Young Boy Confirmed* (London); Contact Pamphlet No. 1,
      "The Days of White Supremacy Are Over," ends 1st series
      "The Long View" (January); returns to work on *Hofmeyr.*
1960 State of Emergency declared in South Africa on March 30;
      takes up duties of Peter Brown, imprisoned National Chair-
      man of Liberal Party; "The Long View," 2nd series (re-
      placing Peter Brown), April to August; "The Third Force,"
      Presidential Address to the Liberal Party (*Contact,* June);
      The Charlestown Story; received the Freedom Award for

1960 from Freedom House, New York; public lectures in London; passport withdrawn on return home; *Mkhumbane* (*Village in the Gulley*), libretto for a musical with music by Todd Matshikiza, performed in Durban before audiences of all races during the tense last week in March following the Sharpeville tragedy.

1961 Collection of short stories entitled *Tales From a Troubled Land* (New York) and *Debbie Go Home* (London); Award from Free Academy of Art, Hamburg.

1962 Hon. degree, Doctor of Letters, Kenyon College; *Sponono* (with Krishna Shah) produced in Durban and Johannesburg.

1963 "The Abuse of Power," Presidential Address to the National Congress of the Liberal Party (*Liberal Opinion,* September.)

1964 *Hofmeyr* published in Cape Town (December); Broadway production of *Sponono;* "The Long View," 3rd series, begun in *Contact;* appeared in the Rivonia Sabotage Trial to plead for mitigation because he feared the defendants would be sentenced to death; "Liberals Reject Violence," Presidential Address to the Liberal Party (*Liberal Opinion,* October).

1965 *South African Tragedy: The Life and Times of Jan Hofmeyr* (U.S. edition of *Hofmeyr*); *Sponono,* published in New York; "The Long View," 3rd series, continued.

1966 Defence and Aid Fund banned; "The Long View," 3rd series, continued; *Contact* reduced to mimeographed sheets once monthly; B.Ed. degree, with distinction, officially conferred by University of South Africa on the basis of M.Ed. program partially completed in 1934; Dr. Hendrik Verwoerd, Prime Minister of South Africa, assassinated; Balthazar J. Vorster succeeds him.

1967 *The Long View* (New York); July 30, delivered farewell tribute at the funeral of his friend Chief Albert Luthuli, the 1960 Nobel Peace Prize winner.

CHAPTER 1

The Evolution of a South African

I A First Novel

FOR more than ten years Alan Paton has led the small, beleaguered South African Liberal Party in opposing his country's racial policy of *apartheid;* yet whenever his name appears in the international press in this political context, it is almost always accompanied by the identifying phrase "author of *Cry, the Beloved Country.*" Since the book and the man are so inevitably associated, and since the book has been for so long the world's window on South Africa, it would be inappropriate to begin any account of Alan Paton without simultaneous reference to his masterpiece.

Paton was born in the British colony of Natal in southern Africa in 1903, but to the world at large his history as a literary man began forty-five years later with the publication in New York of his first novel, *Cry, the Beloved Country.* Unheralded prior to publication, this novel had a small advance sale of about three thousand copies, yet before the year 1948 was out it was acclaimed by critics and by the reading public alike. Rarely, indeed, has a first novel by an unknown writer achieved such popularity, or succeeded in retaining so large a measure of that popularity with the passage of time. In the United States, reviewers were almost unanimous in praising the refreshing simplicity of the novel's language and the deep humanity of its theme. In Britain, after later publication, *Cry, the Beloved Country* was equally widely read and admired. In the Union of South Africa, the "beloved country" of the title, it had a mixed reception; yet it reportedly outsold all other books with the sole exception of the Bible.

Soon after publication, *Cry, the Beloved Country* also reached a variety of audiences through dramatic adaptations and through translations. In 1949, it was adapted for the Broadway stage as the musical, *Lost in the Stars,* by Maxwell Anderson and Kurt Weill.[1] During the next year it was filmed, partly on location in

South Africa, by Alexander Korda.[2] It was later adapted as a
verse drama by Felicia Komai.[3] The novel itself soon achieved
world-wide circulation through translation into some twenty languages in Europe, Asia, and Africa—with the Spanish and Portu-
guese editions widely distributed in Latin America.[4]

Widespread popularity is not always a good gauge of a book's
literary merit. But *Cry, the Beloved Country*'s range of appeal
belies the conviction, dear to some, that popularity and literary
merit should be measured in inverse ratio. What its reception and
continued appeal clearly illustrate is that *Cry, the Beloved Country* shares that quality of universal interest that always distin-
guishes outstanding products of the creative imagination. Some
readers valued Paton's first novel for the refreshing combination
of simplicity and lyricism in its language; others valued it most as
a revealing record of South Africa's social and racial situation; and
others again, although perhaps fewer in number, valued it for its
challenge to their own comfortably sterile Christianity.

Such literary success by a man of forty-five may provoke a sense
of loss at the thought of the novels he might have written had he
turned to creative literature earlier. Paton might indeed have
written other novels—perhaps even good ones—for he already
had a substantial reputation as a writer and a speaker in South
Africa where he wrote for professional journals and, fairly frequently, for *The Forum,* a fortnightly journal of liberal opinion.
From his college days on, he had written poetry, and he had
attempted, and discarded, two or three novels of white South African life. Paton set these first novels in the beautiful Natal countryside in the vicinity of Ixopo where he had his first teaching assign-
ment, and to which he introduces us in the opening cadences of
Cry, the Beloved Country: "There is a lovely road that runs from
Ixopo into the hills . . ." But it is part of the purpose of this account of his literary achievement to suggest that, notwithstanding
his technical skill as a writer, Paton could not have produced the
profound work that *Cry, the Beloved Country* unquestionably is,
prior to the time he began work on it during a visit to Trondheim,
Norway, in 1946. He might have written other books, but not
this book.

In the course of a very active and productive life, Paton has
consistently served an ideal of human freedom that goes hand in
hand with personal responsibility. This ideal of personal freedom

emphasizes a man's need to surmount the limitations of ignorance, illiteracy, or inbred prejudice in order to develop his inherent human capacities. As director of a reformatory institution, Paton relied on increasing freedom as his main instrument of reform. A youth committed to the reformatory for habitual theft, for example, would be given training in a useful trade and, at the same time, increasingly exposed to the temptation to steal or to run away. If this exposure to freedom and responsibility succeeded, then on release he would not be simply someone freed from the reformatory, but a free man who had overcome the habit of stealing and gained the capacity for independent self-support. Again, the South African Liberal Party which Paton has led for a decade describes its ideal, not as integration of the races, but as a nonracial society, that is, a society whose members have freed themselves from inbred racial prejudices.

All of Paton's writings, from those of his student days at Natal University College, 1920–24, to his great biography of Jan Hofmeyr forty years later, express this consistent concern for the freedom, dignity, and worth of individual human beings. The central conflict in his fiction, both within individual characters and in society at large, suggests a confrontation between the positive Spirit of Liberty and the negative Spirit that Denies. In the specific South African settings of his creative works, this encounter frequently appears as an intellectual or spiritual quest in which some characters venture out beyond the restraining bounds of exclusive loyalty to a group, a nation, or a race, and seek to assume the responsibilities of shared humanity.

In *Cry, the Beloved Country,* for example, this theme is developed in the "Private Essay on the Evolution of a South African" found among the papers of the murdered man, Arthur Jarvis. This essay commences: "It is hard to be born a South African. One can be born an Afrikaner, or an English-speaking South African, or a coloured man, or a Zulu." And it goes on to admit: "One can see, as I saw when I was a boy, the reserves of the Bantu people, and see nothing of what was happening there at all" (174). In Paton's most recent work, the biography *Hofmeyr,* this theme of liberation from inhibiting local custom recurs like a refrain: "Hofmeyr was a white South African with white South African fears and prejudices and irrationalities . . . feeling his way out of the bog into which he had been born" (H. 307, S.A.T. 241).

Furthermore, the aim of the South African Liberal Party which
Paton has described in *Hope for South Africa,* and which he has
led as National Chairman and National President since 1956, is to
nurture growth in the Spirit of Liberty. Beyond purely social or
political considerations, this insistent theme of aspiring towards a
non-racial attitude reflects Paton's conviction that genuine Christianity respects the social significance and personal dignity of all
men. He has observed: "I am no theologian or philosopher. I am a
native of Africa, though a white one. I am a Christian, though
falling short of what a Christian should be. Because I am a Christian I am a passionate believer in human freedom, and therefore
in human rights." [5]

Paton's deep respect for the worth and human dignity of all
persons has been taken by spokesmen for the extremes of right and
left in politics as reflecting an outlook either unrealistic or sentimental. An interviewer for the *New Yorker* saw him with a more
perceptive eye as, "not merely a man of good will, but a man of
good will who possesses a lucid, sternly logical mind, whose hu-
manitarianism is unmuddied by sentimentality, and who has as
clear a view of himself as of the world." [6]

II *Natal Childhood and Family Influences*

At the time of Paton's birth in 1903, the "beloved country" of his
first novel did not yet exist as a nation. He was born in Natal
shortly after the end of the prolonged and bitter Anglo-Boer War,
1899–1902. This war was waged by the forces of the British Empire, including those of the colonies of Natal and the Cape of
Good Hope, against the two independent "Afrikaner" or "Boer"
republics of Transvaal and Orange Free State. These Afrikaner
republics had been established by the white South African settlers
of Dutch origin who trekked inland from the Cape to avoid British rule during the 1830's. Until Paton was seven years old, Natal
continued its separate existence as a British colony; then, in 1910,
the four territories—the former British colonies of Natal and Cape
of Good Hope and the former Afrikaner republics of Transvaal
and Orange Free State—came together to constitute one nation,
the Union of South Africa.

Paton's birthplace, Pietermaritzburg, had been originally
founded by the Afrikaner Voortrekkers, and named to commemo-
rate two of their leaders, Piet Retief and Gerrit Maritz. The Brit-

ish, however, had prevented the setting up of an independent Boer republic in that area in the nineteenth century, and had incorporated Pietermaritzburg into their colony of Natal. During Paton's childhood the town had a particularly British atmosphere. He remembers the red-coated soldiers and military bands parading to mark such formal occasions as the king's birthday. He has recorded that he never heard the Afrikaans language spoken when he was a child, and that he was astonished to discover that the names of the streets in Pietermaritzburg were Afrikaans names. In general, the attitude of the English-speaking inhabitants of Natal towards the Dutch-speaking Afrikaners at the turn of the century is summed up in the thoughts of James Jarvis in *Cry, the Beloved Country* when he recalls that "his own father had sworn that he would disinherit any child of his who married an Afrikaner, . . ." (132)

Paton was born into a family that discouraged this common prejudice. His parents were deeply religious, and he recalls that it was from them he first learned tolerance towards the Afrikaner people and sympathy for their language and culture. He later learned the Afrikaans language and studied its literature and the history of the Afrikaner people, and he points out that "all these attempts to appreciate and understand were strengthened by religious motives." [7]

As a grown man, he demonstrated his desire to share the cultural heritage of the Afrikaner by joining wholeheartedly in the Voortrekker Centenary celebrations in 1938. Although many English-speaking South Africans stood apart from these celebrations, Paton, in common with the Afrikaner celebrants, grew a beard and set out for Pretoria in an ox-wagon flying the flag of the Transvaal republic. [8] Years after this symbolic trek, writing of the position of the Afrikaner nationalist in *South Africa Today* (1951), Paton remarked: "I feel for him deeply and painfully. That is why, for example, I never use hurtful language in speaking of Nationalist policies." [9]

The spirit of tolerance that marks Paton's mature attitudes was, as he says, fostered in his home. But it was nurtured, too, by broader South African aspirations. For he grew up in the newly founded Union of South Africa during the great experiment in reconciliation between the English-speaking and Afrikaans-speaking white South Africans, led by the former Boer generals, Louis

Botha and Jan Smuts, that followed the formation of the Union of
South Africa in 1910. Louis Botha's policy of bringing together
South Africans of both English and Dutch origin in a single
shared patriotism, or South Africanism, prevailed, although with
opposition and setbacks, until 1948. On both sides there were substantial groups of dissenters. On the one hand there were the pro-
British, chiefly in Natal, who did not bestir themselves to embrace the culture or language of the Afrikaners; and on the other,
the militant Afrikaner nationalists, chiefly in the Transvaal, who
looked forward to re-establishing the racial policies of the Boer
republics.

Paton's second novel, *Too Late the Phalarope,* is set in the atmosphere of these contending views. The patriarch Jakob van
Vlaanderen is a staunch Afrikaner nationalist, while his son, wife,
and sister prefer a common South African patriotism that supports, for example, South African participation in World War II.
As the narrator, Tante Sophie, explains: "My brother said it was
an English war, and he would not believe the stories of Hitler and
the Jews; but his wife and I were for the English, as we have always been in our hearts, since Louis Botha and Jan Smuts made
us so." (33) Most South Africans who sought a common patriotism after the Union was formed, supported Louis Botha's ideal of
reconciliation. So, too, did Paton; but he expanded his view of a
common South African patriotism to include not only the two
white groups of English and Dutch descent, but also the native
Africans, the people of Indian origin, and the Cape Colored people. It is just such a common patriotism that the South African
Liberal Party under Paton's leadership has proposed as an alternative to the policy of total separation of races in South Africa.

Other childhood influences were also to have lasting effects.
Paton's parents, besides setting his feet on the road to tolerance
and inculcating in him their own religious principles, sparked his
interest in both education and creative literature through their example. His mother was a teacher before her marriage, and his
father, a civil servant who came to Natal from Scotland shortly
before the Boer War, aspired to be a poet. Paton, wryly summing
up his father's dedication to principles and to poetry, has described him as "a strict man and a frustrated poet." [10] Paton himself began writing poetry while still a schoolboy. When he entered
Natal University College at the age of seventeen, he already had

considerable facility in writing verse. Although he was a science
major, and took his Bachelor of Science degree with distinction in
physics, he had broad cultural interests as an undergraduate. He
was active, for example, in university dramatic and literary socie-
ties. He enjoyed writing poetry and soon began to acquire a student reputation as a poet. He was active, too, in the Students'
Representative Council at the time when Leo Marquard (later
one of the co-founders of the Liberal Party) was forming the National Union of South African Students. It fell to Paton to an-
nounce the formation of this organization, NUSAS, at an international student conference in England in 1924.[11]

III *The Young Poet*

Paton's undergraduate reputation as a poet had a genuine foun-
dation. Between the ages of seventeen and twenty-one he published fifteen poems, two humorous dramas (one of them in
verse), and also some prose, in the *Natal University College Magazine*. Only the two dramas and two or three of the poems fall
into that category commonly found in student literary magazines:
that is, pieces written to amuse or satirize a campus coterie, such
as a literary or dramatic society. The remainder of the poems
share a growing mastery of a variety of lyric forms and a rhythmic fluency unusual in a beginning poet. The earliest poems com-
pare quite favorably with the extant youthful poems of many
poets of established reputation.

These poems manifest varied moods and subject matter, but,
with two exceptions, they give no hint of the writer's African
background. Like the poems of all beginning poets who attempt
traditional forms, they are imitative of those poets who have used
these forms; even in mood and subject they fit into the English
anthology alongside the poets Paton admired. In reading them,
one is conscious of Keats, Hardy, or Browning hovering in the
background—and the prevalence of dramatic monologue frequently evokes the latter—rather than of a local sense of some
South African theme or setting. What these poems do show, however, in addition to a fluent facility with language, is a sense of
what technically constitutes a line of poetry quite rare in beginning poets. They also reveal Paton's fine ear for rhythm, and his
sense of "plot," or the ability to unfold a story with economy.

The earliest of these poems is the sonnet, "To a Picture," [12]

which Paton published under the pen name "UBI" when he was
seventeen. Besides showing his considerable facility with the Pe-
trarchan form, it also reveals his typical preference for dramatic
characterizations as subject-matter:

> He gazes on me with his long-dead eyes,
> And dumbly strives to tell me how he died,
> And shows the hilt-stabbed dagger in his side;
> I see mad terror there; the murd'rous cries
> Draw near—more near—half-tottering he tries
> To reach the door—one step!—"unbar, 'tis I."—
> But none unbar—I hear the broken cry,
> I see the mirrored anguish in his eyes.
> So conjure I the tale; the faded print
> Hangs on the bedroom wall, and there I see
> Those wild eyes ever gazing on my bed.
> They lead me to strange wonderings; what hint,
> What sign, what tragic muteness will there be
> In mine own eyes, when they do find me dead?

The following year, at eighteen, he published, and acknowledged
by signing them, a pair of sonnets[13] contrasting in metrical pace
that show a marked advance in formal skill over "To a Picture."
The first is lyrically musical:

> Far out the waves are calling, Marguerite,
> And listlessly they wander to and fro . . .

The second is a dramatic monologue, imitative of Browning; and,
indeed, since Paton's writing at this time displays flashes of sharp
wit, even an intentional parody of Browning. This sonnet, "Give
me my sword—and gird it on, my son," is spoken by an aged,
sightless warrior who recalls his prowess in battle through touch-
ing the hacked edge of his sword blade:

> This dint? That was the crest old Guntrum wore,
> Shouting, "Hast prayed?"—old Guntrum prayed no more,
> I clove him to the horse he rode upon.
> 'Tis broken here; some fool lord with a sneer
> On his fool face, couched lance and rode on me.
> We met and shuddered as two mighty ships
> That meet in fog at night in some dark sea.
> What sayest thou, son? Poor fool didst thou not hear?
> Could my lord sneer, when my lord had no lips?

Another pseudonymous early poem, with loping rhythm and chiming rhymes, may illustrate that pleasure in the sheer musicality of language that never seems to have deserted Paton. This poem, "The Sea," [14] apparently derived from Poe's "The Bells," has fifty-two lines of which the following are a sample:

> Yet they're treach'rous are the billows of the sea.
> They are cold and green and cruel under night's black
> > driving skies,
> As savagely they ravage at the rampart that defies,
> With a cold and cruel crooning o'er the wretch
> > that by them dies,
> Miserably.

In two poems written in his eighteenth and nineteenth years, Paton steps out from the purely literary confines of the English anthology on to the landscape of Natal. The first, "Ladysmith (Midnight on the Battlefields)," is dated, "Ladysmith, July 13th, 1921." [15] It is an elegiac lyric in the manner of Housman, addressed to a young soldier killed near the town of Ladysmith where the Boer forces besieged the British during the Boer War. The emotion in the poem is directed not toward the cause of either warring party, but to the fallen young soldier who, significantly, is not identified as either Boer or British. The sixth and final quatrain, beginning like all the others with the refrain "Art lonely, son?", runs as follows:

> Art lonely, son? the moon will pale,
> And o'er the hills come Dawn for thee,
> See, son, these wild veld-flowers I take
> And twine them on the cross of thee.

The second poem set in the Natal landscape is a ballad of a night train: "Song of the Northward-Bound." [16] This ballad of a lonely camper in the veld, composed in a pattern of ten well-paced, four-, five-, and six-line stanzas, is set in the vicinity of Colenso, scene of a battle where the Boer forces defeated the British in Natal under General Buller:

> Aye, oft in the hills of the thorn-tree belt
> I have heard the Northbound call.

> But where they sleep on the lonely veld
> It sounds the saddest of all.
>
> Dark, and a wind that rustles by me
> In the mist of a weary rain.
> Dark, and the dead that sleep by me
> In the sleep of Colenso plain.

Here again, as in "Ladysmith," the recollection of the Boer War raises no hint of provincial patriotism to Natal.

Two other poems in contrasting style that appeared together in Paton's final year at college will serve to illustrate the range he attained in versification. The first of these is a religious sonnet, "I saw them playing with their bauble, Earth," which has affinities to Hardy's poetry in situation and imagery. It has three characters, Plague, Death, and Mammon, let loose on earth. But it concludes with the lines:

> And while I watched them, lo! a Fourth there came
> And snatched their bauble from each clutching hand,
> Then loud as thunder, "This is mine," He said.[17]

Set side by side with this cosmic drama there is a fragile lyric, "Gemellia," [18] with six quatrains beginning:

> Once in the long dark hours of sleeping
> I woke, and the dawn-wind spoke to me,
> And told me there was a woman weeping
> Down in the pines by the sea.
>
> So I went to the pines in the dawn-wind's blowing
> Coldly and keenly over the sea,
> Pale in the East, and long hair flowing,
> Gemellia passed by me.

In summary, these undergraduate poems attain fine qualities of technical excellence. The world they make manifest, however, bears little resemblance to the world of Paton's later poems and fiction. The heritage they reflect is that of someone immersed in the English writers, particularly those of the late nineteenth and early twentieth century, whose work was more or less contemporary at that time. For a Natal-born young man of British descent, they show exceptional restraint and tolerance when they advert to the Boer War; but, interestingly enough, they are silent on the theme of tribal African life, even though their author had frequently hiked and camped in the vicinity of Zululand and scattered African tribal reserves. In this regard, the lines already quoted from Arthur Jarvis' "Private Essay on the Evolution of a South African" in *Cry, the Beloved Country* are evocative: "One can ride, as I rode when I was a boy, over green hills and into great valleys. One can see, as I saw when I was a boy, the reserves of the Bantu people and see nothing of what was happening there at all . . . It is only as one grows up that one learns there are other things here than sun and gold and oranges." (132)

IV *The Active Life*

Although Paton was not drawn to African or Indian life in Natal as a subject for his undergraduate poems, he records that it was during his years at the university that he began to understand and sympathize with African and Indian aspirations. He was an active member of two student organizations seriously concerned with the problems of justice in South African society as a whole. These were the non-denominational Students' Christian Association and the public-spirited Student Representative Council.

In 1924 the students of his university selected Paton to represent them at the first Imperial Student Conference, held in England at London and Cambridge. His letters from this conference to the Student Representative Council substantiate his tolerant outlook and even his championship of tolerance in matters of race. Two of his letters were published in the *Natal University College Magazine*. The first of these is devoted to the future relations between the English-speaking and Afrikaans-speaking groups in South Africa and is optimistic about the role of student organizations in helping "to weld the whites of South Africa into one race of South Africans." [19]

His second letter, a report from the conference's Commission on Current Political Affairs, emphasizes the need for retaining the goodwill of India, which was likely to "secede from the Empire unless her wrongs were redressed." This letter describes the students representing India at the conference as "fine, dignified, clever, and in many cases handsome men"—a description calcu-

lated to impress his fellow students in Natal in whose eyes all
Indians were poorly educated laborers. Of his discussions with
Indian delegates regarding their compatriots in Natal he says:
"what they complain of, and as far as I can see, rightly too, is that
chances of improving themselves are denied them; they are given
no chance of higher education . . ." He takes advantage of the
occasion to lecture his constituents on the justice of the views of
the Indian representatives: "After all Natal opinion against the
Indians is in many cases unjust"; and he goes on to declare that
white opinion in Natal needed education on this point, and that
the universities and student unions should take the lead in this. If
the Indian delegates impressed Paton, he apparently impressed
them, too, particularly by introducing a motion that the Rhodes
trustees no longer withhold Rhodes Scholarships from Indians.

On the third racial question, Paton's letter has little to say other
than describing it as "not so urgent." Essentially, what these letters reveal is that Paton shared the views then common among
South African liberals on the relative urgency demanded by South
Africa's several problems of relations among races: first, reconciliation between the two white "races," those who spoke English and
those who spoke Afrikaans; second, particularly in Natal, progress
in the relations between whites and Indians; and third, and much
less urgent, relations between whites and Africans. In Paton's own
case, evolution to the point where he urgently desired to turn this
hierarchy on its head did not take long.

Having fulfilled his duties as delegate to the Imperial Conference of Students, Paton took advantage of his visit to Britain to
visit the habitats or the last resting places of some literary ghosts
who haunt his undergraduate poems. He concluded his final letter
from the conference with the reminder: "Poetic enthusiasts will
writhe when I say I spent some time at the ruins of Tintern
Abbey, slept a night at Ludlow, and am this afternoon going to
Stratford." He toured England and Scotland, chiefly by motorcycle, before returning to Natal to take up his first teaching assign-
ment as a teacher of mathematics at Ixopo High School for white
students.[20]

Ixopo is a small rural community forty miles from Pietermaritzburg in that part of the Natal escarpment that he has described as
it must have appeared to the first Voortrekkers: ". . . here was a
paradisial country, a prodigal endowment of hills and valleys and

rivers and streams, a rich lush grass abounding in flowers and game, a warm air full of coloured birds, a promise of reward and a foretaste of happiness to come." [21] Spurred by this locale and, he now thinks, by the Rogue Herries novels* set in the English Lake District, he undertook two or three novels of white South African life set in the vicinity of Ixopo. He continued to write poetry, too, expressing a variety of moods. He contributed one substantial piece of light verse, "The New Physics," [22] to a Commemoration Number of the *Natal University College Magazine*. This poem succeeds, quite surprisingly, in combining the manner of Alexander Pope with that of Robert Burns.

While teaching at Ixopo, Paton met his future wife, Doris Olive Francis. They were married at St. John's Anglican Church, Ixopo, on July 2, 1928. His acquaintance with, and marriage to, Miss Francis may have attracted him to the Anglican Church of the Province of South Africa, which he adhered to devoutly and actively represented at national and international conferences from that time on. After his marriage Paton returned to Pietermaritzburg to teach at his old high school, Maritzburg College, where he remained until 1934.

For all his lyric "singing" of Ixopo in *Cry, the Beloved Country*, Paton's four years there were not necessarily idyllic. He records, for example, a recollection of his first pay-day, which, one might facetiously suggest, may have sparked his interest in the reform of delinquents: "When I was a young man I drew my first salary and hid it under some clothes in a drawer. That night there was no dinner at the boarding-house, the cook had gone, and so had my salary. I never drew my whole salary again . . ." [23]

Shortly after Paton went to teach at Ixopo High School, his path crossed that of a man who was to have a profound effect on the course of his life both as a writer and as a man of affairs. This was Jan Hendrik Hofmeyr, who became Deputy Prime Minister of South Africa prior to the Nationalist Party election victory of 1948 that heralded the coming of *apartheid* as the official South African policy on race. During the fifteen years between 1949 and 1964, with unavoidable delays and interruptions, Paton worked on the great biography, *Hofmeyr* (published in the United States as *South African Tragedy: the Life and Times of Jan Hofmeyr*). Furthermore, from 1956 on, he undertook the burden of leading

* By Hugh Walpole.

the South African Liberal Party, founded in 1953, to keep Hofmeyr's liberal spirit alive in South African politics.

Jan Hofmeyr was a remarkable man. As a child he was an intellectual prodigy. Hofmeyr entered the university in Cape Town at
the age of twelve, and achieved a brilliant scholastic record there,
and subsequently at Oxford University. His later progress in public life was exceptional. At twenty-two he was a professor of clas-
sics; at twenty-four, president of a university; and at twenty-nine
he was Administrator of Transvaal Province—a position approximately equivalent to governor of a state in the United States. In
1933, at the age of thirty-four, he entered Parliament and was
almost immediately appointed to the Cabinet. At the outbreak of
World War II he joined General Smuts in opposing Prime Minister Hertzog's bid to keep South Africa neutral; and, as wartime
Minister of Finance and Acting Prime Minister, he became "the
brain and power behind the South African war machine."

From his university days in Cape Town and Oxford on, Jan
Hofmeyr had participated in the work of the Students' Christian
Association, including the organization of clubs and camps for
boys. Hofmeyr was an enthusiastic camper; throughout his life he
preferred camping to any other form of vacation. In 1926, Paton,
with two other high school teachers, Reg Pearce and Cyril Armitage, established an annual boys' camp in Natal. This camp, the
aim of which was "to win boys . . . to Christian principles in
life and in society," (H. 136, S.A.T. 98) was an outgrowth of the
earlier founding at Natal University College of a vigorous branch
of the Students' Christian Association. Through common links
with the parent association in Cape Town organized by his friend
Oswin Bull, Hofmeyr came to Paton's second camp at Umgababa,
"and then year after year to the new camp site on the Idomba
River at Anerley, which site he helped the Association to buy and
develop." (H. 136, S.A.T. 98)

Jan Hofmeyr sought to act in public life in accordance with his
Christian conviction of human brotherhood—a difficult and courageous posture to adopt in a society where many were convinced
that God had set the races of mankind apart. Paton admired Hofmeyr's courage: "brave, brave, brave, that was the only word for
him." [24] But he was capable, too, of weighing Hofmeyr's limitations. In a sketch of Hofmeyr that he wrote for *South African
Opinion* in 1936, Paton drew attention to Hofmeyr's lack of ap-

preciation for the beauty of art as distinguished from its moral value: "A work of art as work of art eludes him." Paton then makes a clear distinction between a moral and an artistic purpose that might usefully be kept in mind in relation to his own later novels. Hofmeyr, he says, valued, but did not appreciate, beauty: "he would eradicate slums, and build cities of noble buildings and spacious streets; but with a moral and not an artistic purpose." Paton surmises: "Were he a novelist, he would be unable to capture and set down the poignant beauty of human frailty." [25]

V *Winds of Change in South Africa*

In 1934 Alan Paton fell seriously ill with enteric fever. He spent some eleven weeks in a hospital and a further three months of convalescence by the sea. Normally a very active man, he had time during this period of forced inactivity to think deeply. And there was much afoot in South Africa for a serious man to think deeply about. By 1934 the hopeful progress towards reconciliation between South Africans of British and Dutch origin, envisaged in his letters from the Imperial Conference of Students ten years before, had not only halted; it had begun to go in reverse. The new Prime Minister, General Hertzog, favored a "two-stream" policy that placed particular emphasis on separate schools and universities for those who spoke English and those who spoke Afrikaans, and thereby encouraged the perpetuation of separate national identities among whites of British and Dutch extraction. Beyond Hertzog was the splinter-group of the Purified National Party led by Dr. D. F. Malan, who put the survival and ultimate triumph of the white Afrikaner "race" above any other consideration. In the late twenties, legislation affecting Indians in South Africa had intensified, rather than alleviated, restrictions on this group. Some observers felt that the Hertzog election victory of 1929 had been won by an open and unashamed appeal to color prejudice. Furthermore, Hitler's racist theories emerging in Germany were being welcomed by those in South Africa sympathetic to the idea of a master race, and there were unpleasant indications that anti-Semitism was on the rise.

Yet there were hopeful, even cheerful, signs for Paton to think about. In 1933 Jan Hofmeyr became a cabinet minister responsible for Education, as well as Interior and Public Health, in the new fusion government of Hertzog and Smuts. Hofmeyr, who on questions affecting Indian land tenure and Jewish immigration had stood firmly enough in Parliament to be identified by his opponents as the liberals' champion of Indians and Jews, now began a quiet revolution in the area of children's welfare. The improvements he introduced, since they were to apply impartially to institutions for children of all races and colors, were revolutionary in South Africa. Chief among these improvements was a basic shift in emphasis in the treatment of child offenders, so that reformatory institutions were no longer to be regarded as places of punishment, but as places of education. Hofmeyr took the first step in this direction in 1934, when he transferred responsibility for all reformatory institutions from the Department of Prisons to the Department of Education, and prepared to appoint new personnel to supervise the transformation of the three reformatories—for white, for colored (mixed blood), and for native African offenders—into educational institutions.

Paton feels that his desire to serve society constructively has always been balanced against his literary impulses. He has said on this score: "Indeed it can be said that these two urges, the one to write, the other to do constructive social work, have always been in conflict." [26] Events in his own life and on the national scene during 1934 caused the balance to tip in favor of constructive social work. So the "novels of country life" that occupied him at Ixopo and Pietermaritzburg were laid aside. They would not be taken up again.

CHAPTER 2

With Freedom as an Instrument

I *Diepkloof Reformatory*

DURING his convalescence from enteric fever in 1934, Paton applied for the position of Principal at one of the three reformatory institutions newly transferred to the Department of Education from the jurisdiction of the Department of Prisons. When he received his appointment in 1935, it was to the post at Diepkloof Reformatory, then a crowded, prison-like institution for about seven hundred delinquent African youths ranging in age from ten to nineteen.

This reformatory stood on one thousand acres of farmland on the outskirts of Johannesburg between the white suburb of Willowdene and such African slum townships as Newclare, the place described in *Cry, the Beloved Country* as Claremont, "the garbage heap of the proud city." Claremont was the place where Stephen Kumalo found his sister Gertrude reduced to prostitution and the brewing and selling of illegal liquor. As Kumalo's guide, the Reverend Theophilus Msimangu, described it, Claremont was a place where in the aftermath of a police raid, "you can see the liquor running in the streets. You can smell it, you can smell nothing else in that place." (23)

Apart from his own qualities of mind and spirit, there was little in Paton's background to prepare him for this new experience. The boys he had taught during his years in Ixopo and Pietermaritzburg—in an environment of great natural beauty—were the children of comparatively well-to-do white families. Those now coming under his care were chiefly products of Johannesburg's African slums, habituated to poverty and convicted of crimes ranging from petty theft to rape and murder. Yet he saw the prospect before him as a creative task: "Then in 1935 I went to Diepkloof Reformatory, and that was the end of writing, because the transformation of a virtual prison into a school required all one's creative energy." [1]

37

When he undertook this challenging task of transforming a reformatory into a remedial community, Paton probably did not an-
ticipate a day when Diepkloof Reformatory would survive only
through the medium of his own writings on penal reform and his
later fiction and drama. Portions of *Cry, the Beloved Country,* the
play *Sponono,* and several of his short stories are based on particulars of Diepkloof. But Diepkloof itself no longer exists. It became
what it was, a unique experiment in education, through Jan Hofmeyr's action transferring reformatories for youths of all races
from the Department of Prisons to the Department of Education.
It ceased to exist in 1958, when the government of the day closed
it down and transferred its 800 African inmates to rural Youth La-
bour Camps where they would be trained in farm labor under the
supervision of warders.

Paton had conceived of Diepkloof as a place of education and
rehabilitation based on "increasing freedom, increasing responsibility, increasing privilege, and increasing temptation," for there
could be no proof of the sincerity of the offender's intention to
reform until he could at least resist the temptation to run away
when free to do so. This freedom was arrived at by stages. Newly
committed boys were housed in a general "closed" dormitory. As
soon as they proved themselves trustworthy, they were transferred
to cottages, in groups of six to eight, under the care of a house-
father and house-mother. They received immediate recognition
for good behavior, and "free" boys wore distinguishing badges on
their pockets, as in *Sponono.* Each of these boys, said Paton in
1938, "is allowed the privilege on Saturdays or Sundays to roam
about the very extensive farm which we fortunately have. He
makes three promises to his companions at evensong in which he
says, 'I will not touch any property that does not belong to me; I
will not break bounds; and I will obey all the rules of the
school.'" [2] As a further step in preparing them for re-entry into
free society, these free boys could, in time, have weekend leave to
go home to their families or friends in the Johannesburg area. The
most trustworthy senior boys were permitted to live and work
outside Diepkloof, in placement hostels in Orlando and Jabavu
townships where they paid a small part of their earnings for their
keep. They were encouraged to save the rest for the time of their
release. These older boys had some formal schooling, but they
also learned a trade that would be of use in cities, for Paton be-

lieved that since most of the boys came from an urban environment and would return to it, they should be prepared for such a life.

Since the ages of boys committed to Diepkloof ranged from ten to nineteen years, there were different arrangements for the younger and older groups. The younger boys spent their days chiefly in formal schooling. Paton had special affection for these younger ones, and his compassion for them is manifested in his story "Ha'penny" and also his poem "To a small boy who died at Diepkloof Reformatory." [3] Paton repeatedly recommended a separate institution for these smaller boys, for their own benefit, and also to relieve the crowded conditions at Diepkloof. Shortly before he resigned his principalship in 1948, the Department of Education accepted his recommendations to establish a separate school for these younger boys. The money was, in fact, voted for this new school which was to be called the Alan Paton School. But within a month of this decision, there was a change in government in South Africa. Dr. Malan became Prime Minister, and the reformatory for African boys was transferred from the Department of Education to the Department of Native Affairs. The new administration disapproved of the project for the Alan Paton School and it was abandoned.

Within three years of his appointment at Diepkloof, Paton was able to report: "We have removed all the more obvious aids to detention. The dormitories are open all night; the great barred gate is gone." [4] His achievement at Diepkloof was pithily summed up in a catchphrase circulating in Johannesburg that described him as "The man who pulled down the barbed-wire fences and planted geraniums." But not all observers of his experiment shared the indulgent good-will prompting this description. His approach to penal reform had both strong support and strong opposition. And in the end the strength of the opponents prevailed.

The support for his experiments came first from the senior officials in the Department of State responsible for reformatory institutions; and he has recorded that he had the privilege of working for thirteen years under a department "that had tried ably and honestly to give full effect to the provisions of the magnificent Children's Act of 1937." Paton felt that this Act, piloted through Parliament by Jan Hofmeyr, changed reformatory institutions out of all recognition through its basic premise that child-offenders were in need of care, not of punishment. And in his *Hofmeyr* he describes this Act as "one of the most enlightened measures of its kind in the world." Added to his pleasure at the existence of this Act was the unusual freedom permitted him in the practical application of its provisions. He has said on this point: "I even had the extraordinary experience, almost unknown to Public Servants, of administering Diepkloof Reformatory for some years under no regulations at all, and this meant a freedom to experiment that comes to few of us in our lifetime." [5]

He also received another kind of support, invaluable to him in developing his system of restoring offenders to useful and dignified roles in society. This support came from such groups as the South African Institute of Race Relations and its affiliated organization, the Penal Reform League. These groups provided him with platforms for lectures in their symposiums, and the opportunity for writing in the pages of their journals. They also brought out his first two separately published Penal Reform Pamphlets: *The Non-European Offender* (1945), and *Freedom as a Reformatory Instrument* (1948). His pioneering work received similar recognition from the South African liberal fortnightly *Forum*, whose editors commissioned him to prepare a series of articles during 1943 and 1944 on punishment and crime, and the prospects for post-war reform in South Africa.

The chief opposition to Paton's experiments came from the self-righteous observers who believed that crime could be ruthlessly "stamped out." Representatives of this view found Paton's ideas impractical, and his attitude to young offenders sentimental. They preferred their own "realistic" view: that the function of a reformatory—particularly one for delinquent African youths—was to convey, unequivocally, through strictness and deprivation, what Paton calls "the great lesson that crime does not pay." He has noted in his *Hofmeyr* that "one of the sourest observers" of the Diepkloof experiment was Dr. Hendrik Verwoerd, then editor of the newspaper *Die Transvaler*, who described Diepkloof "as a place for pampering rather than education, as the place indeed where one said please and thank you to the black misters." [6] It was Dr. Verwoerd, then Minister for Native Affairs, who closed down Diepkloof and replaced it by a system of rural labor camps in 1958—the same year that he became Prime Minister of South Africa.

II *The Thing to Strive For*

In his early poetry and in those novels "sparked by the Rogue Herries books" that he attempted and discarded, Paton, like many young writers, was taking experience chiefly from literary sources. His later fiction is that of a man who has looked steadily on life. It is marked by a deep, sometimes profound, vision of the irony of the human situation, in which under certain circumstances even a disposition for brutal malice may earn greater approval than reverence for human capacity and worth. His later short stories, "The Waste Land" and "Life for a Life," illustrate this insight to a terrifying degree. It was one thing to delight in the peaceful beauty of the highlands of Natal, and to contrive fictional settings there; but it was quite a different thing to encounter the ugly realities confronting those, particularly Africans, who sought to adapt themselves to the new industrial world taking root in Africa.

In his practical work in social welfare and penal reform, Paton came to recognize, beneath the surface manifestations of delinquency and crime, the profound human problem of contending good and evil impulses in every man—and in society as a whole. He therefore phrased his response to those who believed that increased freedom was a dangerous instrument of reform in this characteristic way: ". . . much more dangerous is our present unscientific belief that punishment can deter men from evil and incline them to good."[7] This awareness of the capacity for evil, as well as for good, is one of the chief characteristics of his literary work. There are no flatly "heroic" or wholly admirable characters in his fiction. Even Stephen Kumalo in *Cry, the Beloved Country,* whom some commentators have described as "saintly," has his petty weaknesses: a touch of vanity, and a tendency to seek to hurt those who have hurt him. And Pieter van Vlaanderen in *Too Late the Phalarope* has an elusive and enigmatic duality of character compounded of both great strength and great weaknesses.

In the literature of any age or place, the notion of "the hero" implies "the kind of human being who most deserves to be celebrated, remembered, and, if possible, imitated."[8] If no character in Paton's fiction represents the sum of desirable human qualities, his novels nevertheless presuppose certain ideal human qualities. In Paton's social settings, these ideal qualities represent "the highest and best kind of thing to strive for in a country like South

Africa," and in the sphere of religion they represent the full consequences of accepting the Christian duty towards one's neighbor.
Paton's characters may seek their way towards this ideal; or they
may attain or reject these qualities to greater or less degree. But
only one character comes close to epitomizing them—particularly
at the social level—and he is already dead when we encounter
him. This is Arthur Jarvis, the murdered man in *Cry, the Beloved
Country*. What we learn of him from others, the writings he has
left behind, and the account of his funeral that draws mourners of
many races, creeds, and social organizations—all these represent,
in summary form, "the highest and best kind of things to strive for
in a country like South Africa."

In short, the ideal man in Paton's novels incorporates qualities
of heart and mind that found practical expression in South Africa
in such pursuits as the work of the Institute of Race Relations, or
in the devotion to the spirit of liberty represented by the journal
Forum, or in the practical Christianity represented by the mis-
sions of the Anglican Community of the Resurrection on which
the Mission House in *Cry, the Beloved Country* is modeled. Some
account of his association with these groups may illuminate a
number of themes in his novels as well as the attitude of mind that
led him to devote his energies to the cause of a non-racial Liberal
Party.

The Forum, founded in 1938, was a South African journal of
opinion that supported Jan Hofmeyr's liberal views. Paton remembers its first appearance as "an exciting event"; and his excitement carries over into his description some twenty-five years
later in *Hofmeyr* where he says: "The first appearance of *Forum*
on 4 April 1938 was an exciting event. It was a challenge to the
whole Malanite creed with its isolationism and racial exclusive-
ness . . . The very cover was exciting. . . . Its pages were large
. . . full of good stuff, and all for sixpence." [9] In editorial policy,
Forum stood for freedom of thought and speech, and "the fearless
expression of opinions by others"; it stood for a broad South Africanism, as opposed to separate and exclusive loyalty to an Afrikaans-speaking or an English-speaking group; and it also stood
for a gradual extension of voting rights to all races.

Forum immediately opened a debate on the question of faith
and fear so familiar in Paton's writings. The first issue declared
editorially: "We believe that if the Afrikaner were released from

fear for his culture, there would be more chance of a constructive contribution to the Native question." A short time thereafter, *Forum* contained an article by Jan Hofmeyr with the title "Faith, Fear and Politics," in which Hofmeyr compares the attitude of the white South African "realist" with that of the "liberal." The "realist," he says, faced with the numerical preponderance of the native African population, logically enough resorts to "a policy of repression which is based on fear." And Hofmeyr adds: "He fails to see the further fact that fear engenders hatred. . . ." Over against this "realist," Hofmeyr sets "the much-abused liberal" who asserts "the essential value of human personality as something independent of race or colour." [10]

The keynote of the first *Forum* editorial—the theme of going forward in faith, and not in fear—which is developed further in Hofmeyr's article, "Faith, Fear and Politics"—is one of the basic themes in Paton's writings. In *Cry, the Beloved Country*, the African priest, Msimangu, repeatedly echoes Hofmeyr's point that fear engenders hatred: "I have one great fear in my heart," Msimangu says, "that one day when they are turned to loving, they will find we are turned to hating." This theme of going forward in faith, not fear, is also at the heart of Arthur Jarvis' "Private Essay on the Evolution of a South African." One should note, too, that what *Forum* and Hofmeyr were proposing for South African society at large is related, by analogy, to what Paton was practicing in the little world of Diepkloof: putting his faith in freedom, rather than repression, as an instrument for restoring warped lives to the fullness of human dignity.

This theme of restoration pervades all of Paton's work. In *Cry, the Beloved Country*, Msimangu says of the breakdown of tribal codes of conduct in the social melting-pot of Johannesburg: "The tragedy is not that things are broken. The tragedy is that they are not mended again." (25) And it is largely on the basis of the insights he gains through conversation with Msimangu that Stephen Kumalo attempts to restore the village of Ndotsheni. Again, in *Too Late the Phalarope*, the police captain, Massingham, says to Tante Sophie: ". . . an offender must be punished, *mejuffrou*, I don't argue about that. But to punish and not to restore, that is the greatest of all offences." (264)

In Paton's series of six articles on crime and punishment published in *Forum* during 1943–44, the pervading stress is on restoration. This series proposes that the best way to deter crime is to restore to each person a feeling of social significance: "To mean something in the world is the deepest hunger of the human soul, deeper than any bodily hunger or thirst, and when a man has lost it he is no longer a man . . ." [11] Another great way to combat crime, according to this series, is to reform society itself, so that every man can take his place in it with dignity:

There is one supreme reason why men do not commit crime and that is because they have goals, interests, ideals, homes, children, savings schemes. The home, the church, the association, have given them worthy aims and have expressed—and continue to express—social approval of their lives and actions. They do not commit crime—not because they are afraid—but because they are socially significant. [12]

If we turn from this assertion to the account of Arthur Jarvis' funeral in *Cry, the Beloved Country,* and note the number of representatives, and the messages of condolence, from the many groups and associations he participated in actively in both the white and black communities, we may observe how the "good" man in Paton's novels is one who works in practical ways to contribute fullness, meaning, and greater social significance to the lives of others.

One important organization in Johannesburg working towards this end was the South African Institute of Race Relations, the most notable organization in South Africa devoted to racial understanding, in the work of which Paton has taken active interest for many years. Founded in 1929, the Institute soon established a fine reputation for intellectual honesty, chiefly through the efforts of Professor Alfred Hoernlé and his wife Winifred, J. D. Rheinallt Jones and his wife Edith, Senator William and Mrs. Margaret Ballinger, M.P., Leo Marquard, and other liberals. Paton defined the aims of the Institute in this way: "while its task was to gather and disseminate objective information about all racial affairs, it was to be done from the point of view of those who believed in a common South African Society, and who regarded segregation as both impossible and unjust." [13]

It may have been partly through his association with the Institute of Race Relations during his years at Diepkloof that Paton became increasingly aware of the difference between intellectual

adherence to principles of racial justice and what he came to understand as a wholly "non-racial" attitude, that is, an attitude
transcending the categories of race or color and recognizing a
common humanity as the basis for one's personal relations. This
was a step, Paton knew, that Jan Hofmeyr had not thought of
taking. Speaking of Hofmeyr as a white South African "painfully
inching his way towards emancipation" from white inhibitions,
Paton says: "It is certain that no non-white person ever entered
the Hofmeyr home in the same way that a white person entered
it, to enjoy Mrs. Hofmeyr's teas and pleasant gossip . . ." He then
goes on, speaking first of those prominent husband and wife
teams closely associated with the Institute: "The Ballingers, the
Hoernlés, the Rheinallt Joneses, had overcome many of these inhibitions, and still more had the white people of the left, the
Communists and the strong Socialists, who, even though they held
an incomplete view of man's nature, were not guilty of the white
Christian heresy of judging him by his color and his race." [14]

There is, of course, no single prototype among Paton's ac-
quaintances for the ideal character in his fiction. Hofmeyr, for all
his brilliant clarity of intellect, had little aptitude for social fellow-
ship, or for establishing personal contacts across the boundaries of
race. Yet his example of moral courage—his unflinching championship of the principles of justice—furnishes an essential quality
of the ideal character. So, also, does Alfred Hoernlé, who is mentioned by name in *Cry, the Beloved Country;* and Paton describes
him in his "Author's Note" as "a great and courageous fighter for
justice."

Jan Hofmeyr, Professor Hoernlé, and others may well supply
some of the qualities of the ideal character in Paton's fiction, but
in the particular instance of the characterization of Arthur Jarvis
in *Cry, the Beloved Country* he appears to have had more in mind
certain memories of Mrs. Edith Rheinallt Jones. In addition to her
work for the Institute of Race Relations, Mrs. Jones was active in
such pursuits as directing a hostel for African young women, and
in organizing troops of Wayfarers—the equivalent of Girl Scouts—
for African school-girls. She continued these activities even after
doctors had warned her that the state of her health required that
she forgo all activity. During World War II Paton agreed to drive
her on her inspections of outlying troops of Wayfarers in tribal
villages. On one such occasion, probably the last, they had to

make their final approach to an isolated village on foot—an exertion that caused Mrs. Jones painful distress. But it was not her uncomplaining courage that impressed Paton most on this occasion. It was his realization that the personal friendship between Mrs. Jones and Mrs. Takalani, the African teacher in charge of the village troop, needed none of the conventional surface politeness so characteristic of social contacts across the boundaries of race in a race-conscious country. He says: "At that time my own relations with black people were extremely polite, but I realized that these two had long passed that stage." Theirs was not a friendship between women of different races; but simply a non-racial friendship.

A month later Mrs. Jones died. Her funeral made a very deep impression on Paton, for he felt it provided a momentary glimpse of racial unity in South Africa. He has referred to the emotion he experienced at this funeral on more than one occasion in his writings: in his 1951 Peter Ainslee Memorial Lecture, *Christian Unity,* for instance; and, in greater detail, as the deepest experience of his life, in "A Deep Experience" (1961). It seems reasonable to suggest that the account of the funeral of Arthur Jarvis in *Cry, the Beloved Country,* and of its profound effect on his father, James Jarvis, draws on this deep experience. Paton recalls that St. George's Presbyterian Church, Johannesburg, was crowded for the funeral services of Mrs. Jones: "Black man, white man, coloured man, European and African and Asian, Jew and Christian and Hindu and Moslem, all had come there to honor her memory —their hates and their fears, their prides and their prejudices, all for this moment forgotten." Looking back, twenty years later when socially mixed gatherings of any kind were either illegal or impossible, at "all South Africa reconciled under the roof of this Church," Paton recalls:

As for me, I was overwhelmed. I had seen a vision, which was never to leave me, illuminating the darkness of the days through which we live now. . . . What life had failed to give so many of these people, this woman had given them, an assurance that their work was known and of good report, and that they were not nameless or meaningless. And man has no hunger like this one. Had they all come, no church would have held them all; the vast, voiceless multitude of Africa, nameless and obscure, moving with painful ascent to that self-fulfilment no human being may with justice be denied . . .

In that church one was able to see, beyond any possibility of doubt, that what this woman had striven for was the highest and best kind of thing to strive for in a country like South Africa.[15]

This deep experience occurred in 1944, towards the close of World War II. It bore fruit for Paton as a writer two years later when Edith Rheinallt Jones's lifelong devotion to restoring in others their sense of self-respect and human dignity suggested aspects of the character of Arthur Jarvis in *Cry, the Beloved Country*. But it also deepened his own understanding of the attitude towards his fellow men that he describes as a "non-racial" attitude. He says of the effect of this experience: "I knew then that I would never again be able to think in terms of race and nationality. I was no longer a white person but a member of the human race"; and he sums up the effect of this deep experience on the evolution of his own racial attitudes with the remark: "I had never been militantly white, but now I became militantly non-racial."

Paton had volunteered for military service at the outbreak of World War II, but his offer was turned down on the grounds that his occupation was essential. He nevertheless added numerous voluntary duties to the exacting demands of his work at Diepkloof. Besides his activities for the Institute of Race Relations and such practical endeavors as his assistance to Edith Rheinallt Jones, he joined in the work of the combined YMCA and Talbot House (Toc-H) War Services and became National Chairman of this voluntary organization which provided somewhat similar services for South African combat forces as the combination of the Post Exchange and the Red Cross volunteer workers did for American servicemen. Even though Paton was not directly involved in military action, the war brought him personal tragedy. His only brother, Athol, was killed in the battle El Wak on the Kenya-Somaliland border, December 16, 1940, at the beginning of the campaigns against Italian forces in Somaliland and Abyssinia.

III *Perspective from Trondheim*

Shortly after the war ended, Paton decided to take a leave of absence from Diepkloof Reformatory to undertake a study of penal and correctional practice in Europe and America at his own expense. He set out, therefore, in the latter half of 1946 on an eight months' tour of penal institutions in Britain, the Scandinavian countries, Canada, and New York, Georgia, Colorado, and California in the United States. In *Freedom as a Reformatory Instrument,* he notes that all these countries shared the then accepted South African view that the duty of society towards delinquent children was one of re-education, and that "one travels to learn refinement and improvement of methods already established."

But in the treatment of adult delinquents and criminals he found no similar shared objectives. Penal institutions for adults tended to emphasize either custodial detention or re-education, without achieving a satisfactory synthesis of these aims. Remarking on this unsolved problem of the relationship of freedom and constraint in penal practice he notes, significantly: "It was in fact my interest in this very dilemma that prompted me to undertake my visits." He found that the most successful attempt at synthesis was being made in Sweden, and that most of the reforms he saw outside Sweden "are reforms within the framework and custody and leave out of account the importance of freedom and responsibility as the supreme reformatory instruments." [16]

Since he undertook this tour unaccompanied, he frequently found himself alone on long journeys or in hotel rooms, particularly in the Scandinavian countries where he did not know the language. It was in these circumstances that the urge to write creative fiction returned. So at Trondheim in Norway he began to write *Cry, the Beloved Country.* He continued working on it in Norway, Sweden, England, and the United States, for the most part in hotel rooms. He finished it some three months later in San Francisco.

CHAPTER 3

Of Fear and Faith:
Cry, the Beloved Country

I *The Plain and Simple Truth*

IN *Cry, the Beloved Country: A Story of Comfort in Desolation*, Paton succeeds to a remarkable degree in portraying a segment of South African life during a brief period immediately following the end of World War II. And he succeeds, to an even more remarkable degree, in endowing this regional portrait with universal significance. He accomplishes this by incorporating into the actualities of South Africa's physical and social setting a fundamental theme of social disintegration and moral restoration. This theme is worked out through two complementary, or counterpointed, actions: Stephen Kumalo's physical search for his son Absalom, and James Jarvis' intellectual search for the spirit of his son Arthur. In each case, the journey, once undertaken, leads to an inner, spiritual awakening.

Yet the story that sustains these deeper themes and contrasts is a very simple one. Stephen Kumalo, aging Zulu pastor of a small Anglican mission church in the tribal village of Ndotsheni, sets out for the unfamiliar world of industrial Johannesburg to seek his sister Gertrude, who had gone there, years before, to look for her husband and had not been heard from again. He hopes also to discover his son Absalom, who went to look for Gertrude and failed to return. And he has the further hope of finding his brother John, who, like so many from the village, had gone to Johannesburg and had not returned. He finds all three. But each is enmeshed in a web of moral degeneration, and his hopes of reuniting them in the old close-knit tribal family are defeated.

He finds his son Absalom a confessed murderer. The victim is Arthur Jarvis, a young white man noted in Johannesburg for his devotion to the cause of racial justice, and the only son of James Jarvis, the white farmer whose land occupies the comparatively

fertile high ground above the barren and eroded valley of Ndotsheni. During the time that elapses between the discovery of the
murder and the completion of the trial, the paths of the bereft
fathers cross. Each seeks to understand his own son and to discover the root causes of his divergence from accustomed ways—
the one fallen from the standards of the church his father served,
the other committed to a vision of racial justice quite alien to his
father's conventional assumptions. The older men return to their
homes, like T. S. Eliot's Magus, "no longer at ease in the old dis-
pensation." Although neither can hope to have his son restored to
him, their mutual recognition of each other's suffering engenders a
hitherto unthought-of sense of neighborhood, and of shared humanity.

The simple narrative framework of this story is, in itself, no
creative triumph. It can achieve literary significance only to the
degree that Paton matches the depth of his vision with the artistic
power to orchestrate the initial mood and literal statement to their
fullest potential.

Every novelist, while engaged in composition, struggles to rec-
oncile a desire to represent some human situation truthfully, with
a desire to arrange his materials in the best, and most interesting,
order. For some writers, the technical matters of style and arrangement are a primary concern. Others, impelled by the urgency of their concern with the human situation, adopt fictional or
dramatic forms as their medium of expression. *Cry, the Beloved
Country* is a product of this second urge, which Paton once described as a desire to write "books that would stab South Africa in
the conscience." Yet it is also a successful artistic achievement.
Paton draws attention to the moral aspect of his purpose in his
"Author's Note" on fictional persons and events, when he states:
"In these respects therefore the story is not true, but considered as
a social record it is the plain and simple truth." (vii)

In the light of the broad facts of the South African social record
in 1945–46, the period of the novel's setting, this claim is certainly
justified. Even those who did not share Paton's views on race relations would admit that the conditions encountered by the aged
Zulu priest, while searching for his son, really existed. It was true
that the land in tribal reserves, like the countryside around his
tribal village, Ndotsheni, was poor, badly eroded, and unable to
sustain its people; that the tribal reserves were inhabited chiefly

by old men and women because the young men were away working in the mines and the industries of Johannesburg; and that conditions in overcrowded African townships, and lack of opportunity for employment, contributed to growing frustration and crime.

There seems little doubt, therefore, that Paton turned to literary creation again, not out of nostalgia for the creative pursuits of his youth, but impelled by the urgency of what he had to say about social and moral disintegration in South African society. An article of his that appeared in *Forum*, December 15, 1945, almost on the eve of his departure for the tour of Europe and the United States during which he wrote *Cry, the Beloved Country,* is of particular interest in this connection, for it shows that the basic theme of the novel was uppermost in his mind. This brief article, "Who is Really to Blame for the Crime Wave in South Africa?",[1] is remarkable for two reasons: first, for the urgency of its tone; and second, because it contains the essential themes of *Cry, the Beloved Country,* prior to their embodiment in fictional form. This article treats two major aspects of the social condition of Africans, namely, the problems of disintegration and the need for restoration.

Paton begins by warning against the tendency to dismiss outbreaks of crime among Africans as part of a general post-war phenomenon, thereby ignoring the more important cause, the disintegration of tribal society under the impact of Western economy and culture. "For a long time," he says, "the full dangers were not seen, but fathers and sons and daughters went to work and sometimes never came back. . . ." In the course of time, Africans attempted to set up new homes in cities, but, robbed of the powerful support of tribal custom, these families "began to experience with bewilderment and shame the shocks of disobedient children, pregnant daughters, delinquent sons." The atmosphere of overcrowded slums accelerated this decay of home life which, he says, also decayed in the tribal reserves, "where men did not come back, and where women went away to look for them and often found someone else." This is, essentially, the picture of disintegration incorporated into Book One of *Cry, the Beloved Country.*

The second part of the article turns to the question, "How is society to be restored?" And it responds: "Moral and spiritual decay can be stopped only by moral and spiritual means." Restoration requires education and opportunities for work and the growth of self-respect so as to create a climate where decency and morality can flourish. He repeats the insistent theme of his earlier *Forum* articles: "Men obey the laws when they are pursuing worthy goals, working for some good purpose, making the most of their seventy years, using their gifts."

At this point he turns to the theme of fear in South African society at large that reverberates through *Cry, the Beloved Country*. He adverts to that unacknowledged fear causing white society to deny Africans the right to develop their potential gifts in almost all trades and occupations above the level of menial tasks. "It is these gifts of which we are afraid," he says, "and as long as we fear them we shall be at the mercy of other more terrible gifts developed in the school of poverty, ignorance and cunning."

When Paton incorporated these views into his portrait of South African society in *Cry, the Beloved Country*, he could justifiably claim that his novel "considered as a social record was the plain and simple truth." He was well aware of the statistics of the social record, and he was accustomed to marshaling the evidence before public and private bodies. In his address to the National Social Welfare Conference in September, 1944, for example, he set up his evidence for the causes of the disintegration of family life in the form of an elaborate diagram. His views on this subject were far from being personal or eccentric. Many educators, welfare workers, missionaries, and even government commissions had frequently made similar estimates. He had, therefore, little reason to doubt the authenticity of his picture or to underestimate the urgency of his cause.

Besides focusing on the general climate of disintegration, *Cry, the Beloved Country* draws on many other facets of the South African social record of 1945–46. In this respect it is typical of Paton's fictional method, which, characteristically, seeks materials in the actualities of South African life. There are specific public events like the building of Shanty Town, the bus boycott, the discovery of rich new gold deposits at Odendaalsrust, and the air of frenzied excitement that the discovery engendered on the Stock Market and in Johannesburg as a whole. The actual record also included such less publicized endeavors as the work of the Anglican clergy, both black and white, at the Mission House, Sophiatown; and of the welfare workers at Diepkloof Reformatory and at "the wonderful place," Enzenzeleni, where the blind were rehabilitated. According to Professor Horton Davies, Paton relied on his memories of certain actual persons to provide the models for some of the characters in the novel engaged in these humanitarian endeavors. He says, for example, that Father Trevor Huddleston of the Rosettenville Mission House of the Anglican Community of the Resurrection provided the model for the sympathetic portrait of Father Vincent, that the young welfare worker from the reformatory was modeled on a Probation Officer at Diepkloof, and that "the physical outline of Kumalo was provided by an old man who used to visit Diepkloof Reformatory." Professor Davies goes on to identify Arthur Jarvis with Paton himself: "The wide interests of the man and the very titles of his cherished library and the significant portraits on the wall of his study, these are as autobiographical as the social Credo and the ethical platform of Alan Paton." [2]

Undoubtedly Arthur Jarvis' library, with its books on birds and flowers as well as on race relations and literature, is modeled on the author's own collection, for Paton's hobbies include birdwatching and gardening. The wide interests of Jarvis also parallel those of the author, who was himself associated with such organizations as Toc-H, YMCA, the Transvaal Non-European Boys' Clubs, and the Society of Christians and Jews. Yet the character of Arthur Jarvis in *Cry, the Beloved Country* is not simply a self-portrait. As was pointed out in a previous chapter, Jarvis is a representative type, incorporating the admirable traits of a number of people whom Paton felt had found the right road. Nevertheless, Professor Davies' identification of Paton's models substantiates the view that he draws on incidents and persons from actual life for fictional material—a method that adds to the element of authenticity in the novel's social record.

Characteristics of actual persons and events may be more easily modified to fictional purposes than an atmosphere or mood which, while unmeasurable, may nevertheless supply part of the truth of a total situation. Yet *Cry, the Beloved Country* attempts to manifest this aspect of the truth, too, for the novel probes the less tangible but no less real problems of the sensitive, subconscious springs of racial attitudes that, tinged with "the bondage of fear," inhibit the inclination to restore. It reveals one fear in particular, diagnosed by the thoughtful young Zulu priest, Msimangu, who had no hate for any man: "I have one great fear in my heart, that one day when they turn to loving, they will find we are turned to hating." (40) The intensity and pervasiveness of this fear is one of the central themes of the novel. Fear shows in the eyes of the God-fearing as well as of evil-doers. There is fear, too, in the daily newspapers. The land itself is enveloped in fear. And fingers of fear reach toward the future: "Cry, the beloved country, for the unborn child that is the inheritor of our fear. Let him not love the earth too deeply." (80) This intense concern with a climate of fear heightens the basic dramatic conflict of love and hate, for many of the characters know, or come to know, that fear engenders hatred, and that only through love can fear be cast out.

II *The Artistic Object*

It would be difficult to imagine a point on the earth's surface so different in every way from South Africa as Trondheim, Norway. Yet it was fortunate for the artist in Alan Paton that Trondheim was the place where he undertook to compose *Cry, the Beloved Country*. Distance permitted a perspective that allowed him to see his country and the struggles of its diverse peoples as a whole. It is essentially this over-all point of view that makes *Cry, the Beloved Country* a unique artistic object: a dramatic manifestation of the agony of a country in which the spirit of South Africa hovers always on stage and dominates the human actors. It is like the ever-present sea in J. M. Synge's play, *Riders to the Sea*—a threatening and life-giving force that dominates the human action.

It is not surprising that Paton wrote *Cry, the Beloved Country* quickly, since he already had all the material in mind. What is surprising, however, is that he wrote it so well. The stroke of genius that produced a unique artistic masterpiece was his hitting upon a lyric and dramatic framework that could incorporate more than the realistic "slice of life" ordinarily offered by novels of social purpose. From the perspective of Trondheim the whole of South Africa lay before the artist's inner eye like a map. He could envision the beautiful landscape of Natal, and the contrasting bustle of Johannesburg, the City of Gold, a magnet for Africans from tribal areas seeking a new way of life. Even more significant than the landscape spread out before his mind's eye was the din of remembered voices on his inner ear—South African voices talking incessantly about problems—problems of race, problems of language, and problems of separate living space. *Cry, the Beloved Country* is, in fact, a book for the ear rather than the eye. There are many works of art that incorporate a multitude of voices, from Greek tragedy, with its choruses comprising "the voices of the people," through Langland's *Piers Plowman*, with its "field full of folk," or Chaucer's many-voiced Prologue to the *Canterbury Tales*, to James Joyce's medley of tongues in *Finnegans Wake*. What all these have in common is their mingled lyric and dramatic method, for a multitude of voices cannot be incorporated in discursive prose. We may recall in this context, that Paton's early writings showed a marked aptitude for combining lyric and dramatic qualities.

Paton, then, did not superimpose a poetic, or lyrical, prose style on the social theme of his novel; rather he composed the novel of lyric and dramatic elements because, artistically, there was no other way to achieve his aim. Even a cursory examination of this work will show that it is almost free of direct narrative prose. Of its thirty-six chapters, the opening chapter and parts of others are wholly lyrical. The great majority are composed substantially of dialogue that compounds lyric and dramatic elements. Only two—those in which James Jarvis is alone in his son's study—appear to be wholly narrative; yet there is a silent dialogue in these also, between the voice of the dead man speaking through his writings and the thoughts of the father encountering ideas so alien to his own habitual assumptions.

Three artistic qualities of *Cry, the Beloved Country* combine to make it an original and unique work of art: first, the poetic elements in the language of some of the characters; second, the lyric passages spoken from outside the action, like the well-known opening chapter; and third, the dramatic choral chapters that seem to break the sequence of the story for social commentary, but which in fact widen the horizon of the particular segments of action to embrace the whole land, as well as such universal concerns as fear, hate, and justice.

Every reader of *Cry, the Beloved Country* is struck by the simplicity of its language and the rhythmic quality of its prose style. Some of its rhythms, particularly those dependent on parallel phrases and repetitions, evoke the language of the Psalms. Because of this, the style of *Cry, the Beloved Country* has frequently been described as biblical. This description is accurate only up to a point, since it implies that this is Paton's natural style, and that the whole novel is written in one style. The novel has a wide variety of styles; the one that strikes readers first as having a flavor of originality is the suggestion of the rhythms of Zulu speech that appears, chiefly, in Stephen Kumalo's speech and thought, and in dialogue among African characters. Since this occupies a proportionately large part of the novel, it has been, perhaps understandably, taken as the basic style of the whole. For an obvious contrast, however, one should look at the style of the elder Harrison in Book Two. Harrison is almost a caricature of the typical United Party man from Johannesburg's English-speaking commercial community. He parrots hackneyed ideas about "the native problem." He speaks almost wholly in clichés, and is quite incapable of examining them from a fresh viewpoint. He is like the "stone age" neighbor in Robert Frost's "Mending Wall," who cannot go behind his father's saying: "Good fences make good neighbors."

For a stylistic counterpoint to the conventional commonplaces of Harrison's language one should turn to the documents left behind by the murdered man, Arthur Jarvis. In these, anyone familiar with the writings of Alfred Hoernlé—whose spirit frequently walks abroad in the novel—would probably recognize in their trenchant arguments, not only echoes of the ideas, but indications of the personal "synoptic" style that Hoernlé sought to develop.[3] Or again, one might turn to another admirer of Hoernlé, the young Zulu city-bred priest, Msimangu, whose speech, unlike Kumalo's, has a marked quality of clear, logical expression: "The tragedy is not that things are broken. The tragedy is that they are not mended again. . . . It suited the white man to break the tribe. . . . But it has not suited him to build something in the place of what is broken." (25–26) One could pursue these differences further: to the speech of James Jarvis, for instance, or of the white priest from England, Father Vincent, or of the village schoolmaster in Ndotsheni, and find a personal quality in each. The fact is that Paton's ear seems extraordinarily well tuned to the varied rhythms of speech, and that he intentionally uses differences in speech patterns to give individuality to his characters, and to the cacophonous voices that clamor in his choruses.

Even though Cry, the Beloved Country is not written in one style and rhythm but in many styles and rhythms, there is, nonetheless, a dominant style associated with the book. This is the pattern of speech with a marked poetic quality accorded to Kumalo and the African characters generally, and also to some extent employed in the lyric passages voiced from outside the action. This quality can be viewed as an artistic re-creation, in English, of the sound and syntax of spoken Zulu. But to be more precise, it is an artistic amalgam: a melting-pot of African and other speech patterns analogous to the tribal melting-pot in industrial Johannesburg. Thus, the language of *Cry, the Beloved Country* is a poetic invention designed to carry over into English the effects of the sound and idiom of African speech.

At least as many readers were drawn to *Cry, the Beloved Country* by the freshness of its language and the pleasure of its rhythms as by its insights into social dilemmas and complex relations among races. In contrast to the commonplace language of journalism they found Paton's language fresh and lively. What Paton achieves has its closest analogy in the poetic language of J. M. Synge's Irish plays. In both, the "dialect" is a poetic invention. J. M. Synge characterized the language of the naturalistic drama and fiction of his day as "dealing with the realities of life in joyless and pallid works," and proposed an approach to literature which, it seems, Paton's success has substantiated. Both Synge and Paton affirm the value of poetic qualities in literature in strikingly similar ways. Synge declared: "In a good play every speech should be as fully flavoured as a nut or an apple, and such speeches cannot be written by anyone who works among people who have shut their lips on poetry." And Paton, reflecting perhaps on the theme of his novel, has said: "If you write in terms of poetry, fears and inhibitions disappear." [4]

III   *The Voices of South Africa*

Beyond the level of language and syntax, Paton uses another poetic device in *Cry, the Beloved Country* that enables him to extend the horizons of the necessarily limited world experienced by his characters. This poetic element consists of two kinds of chorus. One of these is lyric, and is spoken by a single voice outside the immediate action of the novel. The other is a dramatic medley of voices. Both kinds of chorus permit Paton to make manifest artistically a broad spectrum of events and attitudes, comprising the general complexities of land and people; it is

through them that the Beloved Country itself participates in the
novel. To say this is not to suggest that Paton set out intentionally
to invent a modern instance of the Greek chorus. But it does imply that in attempting to express the broadly national implications
of his theme—which could easily have devolved into unrelated
social commentary—he arrived at a lyric and dramatic technique
analogous to the Greek form that permitted a wide perspective on
the land and people as a whole.

The lyric voice from outside the action is sometimes raised at
climactic moments within episodes; as it is, for example, towards
the close of Chapter 11 where it intones the refrain "Cry, the beloved country. . . ." This refrain rises again during the dramatic
chorus in the next chapter. The most sustained instances of the
lyric voice are the famous passage that forms the opening chapter
of Book One, and the variation upon it that opens Book Two.

The novel opens with a lyric passage beginning: "There is a
lovely road that runs from Ixopo into the hills. These hills are
grass covered and rolling, and they are lovely beyond any singing
of it . . ." (3) The recurrence of identical or slightly varied
phrases in this lyric imposes a pattern resembling verse; it sets up
a contrast between the fertile, well-tended hill farms and the desolate, eroded tribal lands below. Rhythmically, its repetitions have
a kinship with the basic element of repetition in Hebrew poetry
that shows through in good translations of the Psalms, but the
contrasting ebb and flow of the whole more closely resembles the
counter-turn of strophe and antistrophe in a Greek ode. One
might easily envision it recited as the *parados* (entrance chorus)
of a Greek play.

The lyric passage provides an opening for the novel's theme of
the broken tribes and their desolate lands—a principal theme of
Book One. But it proves valuable to Paton again at the opening of
Book Two where the repetition of the first half—the strophe—
serves to introduce the portion of the novel set in the white-owned
fertile uplands; and where, too, the omission of the antistrophe
reinforces the intended contrast. This device of using a variation
on the same passage to mark contrasting settings in a novel is not
unique. George Moore, for instance, used a surprisingly similar
technique in *Esther Waters*, where the passage that opens the
book appears again to introduce the second portion of the novel
set twenty years later.

The second kind of chorus widens the novel's perspective on the land and people as a whole. This choral device occurs in those chapters which may appear, at first, to be social commentary on South African conditions almost crudely interpolated in the main action. There are three such chapters in particular: Chapter 9, which might be called a Chorus of African Voices; Chapter 12, which is, similarly, a Chorus of White Voices; and Chapter 23, which is a mingled Chorus on Justice. A closer reading will reveal a better balance between artistic shaping and social intention; it will also show that these general commentaries are related to the main action of *Cry, the Beloved Country* in a way comparable to the manner in which the role of the chorus in Greek drama is related to the main action.

In a Greek play the main action is represented in a series of confrontations between actors on a raised central stage. Below them in the orchestra, the Chorus, in its turn, generalizes in its commentary the particular confrontation. The Chorus of African Voices in Chapter 9 of *Cry, the Beloved Country* similarly universalizes the theme of Stephen Kumalo's personal agony. On first meeting Kumalo in Ndotsheni, we learn that his close kin, Gertrude, Absalom, and John, have "disappeared" in Johannesburg as have "many other relatives" and "many of his own people." This initiates the theme of the broken tribe from the perspective of Ndotsheni, and Chapter 2 ends with a brief lyric passage on this theme, beginning: "All roads lead to Johannesburg." This theme is intensified in the course of Kumalo's search, and the Chorus of African Voices, in Chapter 9, opens by picking up the refrain: "All roads lead to Johannesburg. If you are white or if you are black they lead to Johannesburg. If the crops fail there is work in Johannesburg." This choral chapter is composed of snatches of anonymous dialogue, brief dramatic confrontations of Africans seeking a place to live in the African townships of Alexandra, Sophiatown, or Orlando. These are frequently interspersed with repetitions of this refrain, or variations on it:

> Have you a room to let?
> No, I have no room to let.
> Have you a room to let?
> It is let already.
> Have you a room to let? (52)

This theme of constant seeking leads, inevitably, into the episode of the building of Shanty Town as a last refuge for homeless squatters. And this Shanty Town episode continues to evolve through snatches of dialogue between African voices, mainly anonymous. The Chorus of African Voices also generalizes the themes of the broken tribes and the Johannesburg melting-pot: "Yes this house is full, and that house is full . . . all coming to Johannesburg." (53) This Chorus of African Voices has immediate relevance to Kumalo's quest also, for it occurs at the point where the search for Absalom leads to Shanty Town.

The second choral episode is a Chorus of White Voices in Chapter 12. This Chorus takes its rise from the episode in the previous chapter where the clergy in the Mission House, including Kumalo, read the newspaper account of the murder of Arthur Jarvis in Parkwold. This gives rise to Kumalo's particular foreboding that Absalom might be among the murderers: "Here in my heart there is nothing but fear. Fear, fear, fear." It also introduces the general theme of fear in the land, a chord that is picked up to open the Chorus of White Voices in Chapter 12: "Have no doubt it is fear in the land." The idea of a chorus of voices is specifically mentioned here, and indeed, becomes a refrain: "There are voices crying what must be done, a hundred thousand voices . . . one cries this, and one cries that, and another cries something that is neither this nor that." (75) This Chorus on fear has three sequences. The first sequence is a series of snatches of dialogue expressing various viewpoints, all concerned specifically with conditions in Johannesburg. For example, voices demanding that crime be "stamped out"—voices recommending that society be reformed. The second sequence is a series of four monologues that widen the perspective to embrace South Africa as a whole. The last of these returns to the particular event from which the chorus as a whole generalizes—that is, the murder of Arthur Jarvis: ". . . for the speaker of the evening, Mr. Arthur Jarvis, has just been shot dead in his house in Parkwold." (80)

The Chorus of White Voices ends here and a brief lyric passage provides a bridge to the frenzied swirl of fear-filled activity that concludes the chapter. The lyric passage repeats the refrain begun at the conclusion of the Mission House newspaper episode: "Cry, the beloved country, for the unborn child that is the inheritor of our fear. Let him not love the earth too deeply." The first upsurge of this refrain in the previous chapter introduced Kumalo's particular foreboding; here his fear becomes a growing, terrifying possibility as he and Msimangu rapidly retrace the steps of their search for Absalom from Sophiatown, to Alexandra, to Shanty Town, to Diepkloof Reformatory, and on to the house of the nameless girl in Pimville; with everywhere the same breathless dialogue:

> Have the police been here?
> They have been here. It was now, now, that they left.
> What did they want?
> They wanted the boy, Absalom Kumalo. (83)

Paton wisely lets the sequence of dialogue express the theme of generalized fear transformed into Kumalo's particular terror. When Msimangu remarks that Kumalo is trembling, the old man responds, "I am cold, very cold"; and Msimangu looks up at the cloudless sky, from which the sun of Africa is pouring down upon the earth. "Come to my room," he says. "We shall have a fire and make you warm again." (85)

There is a third instance where the novel shifts its focus from the immediate story of Kumalo to a wider perspective. This occurs when the specific instance of the administration of justice in Absalom's trial for murder in Chapter 22 moves in Chapter 23 to a general consideration of social justice. The theme of social justice hinges on an actual event of 1946 in South Africa: the discovery of new rich gold deposits at Odendaalsrust in the Orange Free State, an event that occurred about the time of the novel's setting. So the trial scene, which opens with a commentary on justice under the law, is generalized into the broad theme of social justice: "There is little attention being paid to the trial of those accused of the murder of Arthur Jarvis of Parkwold. For gold has been discovered, more gold, rich gold." (167)

Like the other choral chapters, this chapter sets forth attitudes towards its theme of social justice from various perspectives; for example, that of the English-speaking commercial community whose lives revolved around the activities on the Johannesburg Stock Exchange: "And perhaps a great city will grow up, a second Johannesburg . . ."; or an opposing view from the humanitarian-minded: "All the welfare workers and this Father Beresford and the other Kafferboeties say it must not be so, though it must be admitted that most of them haven't one share certificate to rub against another." (171) This chapter differs from the other choral episodes in one respect. It is not presented through the objective medium of lyric drama, but the necessarily subjective medium of satire, aimed chiefly at the English-speaking adherents of the United Party, then in power in South Africa. Here, more than anywhere else, Paton reveals the raw edge of his attitude towards complacent self-centered opportunists impervious to the sufferings of others. This chapter is also a commentary on the theme "power corrupts" that has its specific application in John Kumalo, and it is perhaps the only segment of the novel where the social intention does not achieve perfect balance with the artistic, shaping intention.

IV The Stages of Kumalo's Quest

Apart from its lyric and dramatic medium, Cry, the Beloved Country is composed artistically on the framework of three related quests, or dramatic seeking actions on different planes, corresponding largely to Book One, Book Two, and Book Three of the work itself. Book One, which might be described as the Book of Kumalo, is concerned at first with the physical quest of the Reverend Stephen Kumalo, who travels from the African village of Ndotsheni to Johannesburg in search of his sister Gertrude, his son Absalom, and his brother John, who have all "disappeared" in the metropolis. His guide to these regions of lost people is another Anglican priest, a fellow Zulu of wholly different background, the Reverend Theophilus Msimangu. Msimangu, as has been pointed out, is a man with a deep philosophic bent and clear logical mind whose secular hero was the sharp-witted philosopher Alfred Hoernlé. He guides Kumalo down among the lost people as Virgil guided Dante through the infernal regions, opening his eyes and his understanding to the meaning of enigmatic things. They find Stephen's sister Gertrude, his brother John, and, finally, his son Absalom, only to discover that he is the confessed murderer of Arthur Jarvis.

Book Two is the Book of James Jarvis, father of the murdered man. He sets out from the closed mental world of his own habitual assumptions and prejudices and seeks to understand the liberal spirit revealed to him in his son's reputation and writings. Again, on the analogy of Virgil led by Dante, James Jarvis, "seeking his way out of the fog into which he had been born," is guided by the voice of his dead son who had "journeyed . . . into strange waters" and set down his philosophy in "A Private Essay on the Evolution of a South African."

Book Three is the Book of Restoration. In it, the physical and psychological quests of the earlier books turn toward the spiritual path of redemption. This is the region where, after guiding him through the horrors of hell and the mount of purgatory, Virgil left Dante to proceed alone with no guide but love.

In Book One the reader accompanies the simple man, Stephen Kumalo, on his physical journey to Johannesburg and observes those experiences that open his eyes to the manifestations of good and evil prevailing in this strange new industrial world. Kumalo is robbed, and he is treated with kindness; he visits places of despair like Claremont where he finds his sister Gertrude, and places of hope like Ezenzeleni where the blind are rehabilitated; he witnesses his brother John's self-seeking corruption and Msimangu's selfless dedication; he becomes aware, too, of conflicting good and evil impulses within himself. He is a good man seeking lost sheep, yet he lies to his fellow-travelers on the train to protect his self-esteem; and he is cruel to the nameless girl who is to bear Absalom's child, as he is later cruel to his brother John whose cunning has saved his own son at Absalom's expense.

In Book Two the reader observes James Jarvis' deep experience as he returns again and again to the writings on social justice left by his murdered son. These papers present the case for racial conciliation in South Africa from the Christian and liberal standpoint that Paton shared with Jan Hofmeyr. They open James Jarvis' eyes for the first time to the real plight of both rural and urban Africans—the destruction of their social organization without provision for its replacement by something better: "It was permissible to allow the destruction of a tribal system that impeded the growth of the country. . . . But it is not permissible to watch its destruction, and to replace it by nothing, or by so little, that a whole people degenerates, physically and morally." They also open his eyes to the need for restitution and restoration: "Our civilization has therefore an inescapable duty to set up another system of order and tradition and convention. . . ." (146)

The writings of his son's hero, Abraham Lincoln, guide James Jarvis in deciding the form the memorial to his dead son should take, for he returns more than once to the Gettysburg Address, in which he encounters: "It is rather for us to be here dedicated to the great task remaining before us—that from these honored dead we take increased devotion to that cause for which they gave the last full measure of devotion; that we here highly resolve that these dead shall not have died in vain. . . ." [5]

James Jarvis realizes that his son had journeyed into deep waters, but he also realizes that he must honor and carry forward his son's work as far as it is possible for him to do so. He therefore gives practical financial help to the African Boys' Club and to the drought-stricken village of Ndotsheni. And he learns to respect the sufferings of the old man whose son had murdered his son.

V Book Three: Restoration

The theme of restoration pervades Book Three on several levels. There is a beginning made on the restoration of the land through the work of a young agricultural demonstrator; there is the restoration of Kumalo's leaky village church through the generosity of James Jarvis; and this, in turn, is a halting step towards the restoration of brotherhood—one human being reaching out toward another across the barriers of fear and prejudice. The climax of the theme of spiritual restoration is reached when Kumalo, who in Book One neared despair, makes his lonely pilgrimage to the mountaintop to share his son's bitter agony on the morning set for his execution. In Kumalo's desolation, his only comfort comes from the knowledge of his son's spiritual restoration through the priestly ministrations of Msimangu and Father Vincent.

Book Three, with its aim of evoking a Christian sensibility, may be open to the dual danger of uncritical applause from those who share Paton's Christian faith, and to charges of sentimentality from those who do not. Yet Paton does not permit the reader either to applaud Jarvis' "conversion," or to smile tolerantly on it as a matter beyond the limits of practical sociological concern. At this very point in the novel he appears quite deliberately to raise the question: "What courses of action are the concern of a practical man, and what courses of action are impractical?" His answer ironically contrasts two ways of undertaking the relief of present suffering.

One way is to hope for an ideal, utopian solution through the intervention of some "responsible" agent or impersonal force, such as the state, equipped with blueprints and long-range theories. Another way is, meanwhile, to take those practical steps, however small, that lie within reach. The "good" characters in the novel do not accept evils passively. They act, not only for "humanitarian" reasons, but because as human beings they are involved in mankind, and are in a real sense their brothers' keepers. It is, indeed, a simple personal action—an assumption of the responsibility of priestly brotherhood that opens up the whole Pandora's box: namely, Msimangu's letter to Kumalo informing him of his sister Gertrude's "sickness." Kumalo learns in Johannesburg that he, too, bears a measure of personal responsibility for alleviating suffering; and must *act* like Msimangu, and the people at Ezenzeleni and the Reformatory, and like Dubula who set up Shanty Town. He decides on the unprecedented, if unrewarding, step of seeking an interview with the chief to propose some practical steps to alleviate the suffering caused in Ndotsheni by the drought. And he does this because "the great city had opened his eyes to something that had been begun and must now be continued."

Next he seeks out the headmaster of the local school, where, as the chief reminded him, "we have been teaching these things for many years." There is a fine irony in Paton's portrait of the headmaster that satirizes the impracticality of theoretical schemes. Paton even has a special rocking rhythm that mocks the headmaster: "his office was filled with notices in blue and red and green." When Kumalo sought his advice about practical measures, he was answered in theoretical jargon pitifully far removed from reality: "The headmaster explained that the school was trying to relate the life of the child to the life of the community, and showed him circulars from the Department in Pietermaritzburg, all about these matters. He took Kumalo out into the blazing sun, and showed him the school gardens, but this was an academic lecture, for there was no water, and everything was dead." (233) It is against this background of futile, high-sounding schemes and theories that Jarvis' simple, practical act of providing milk for the sick children is set with purposeful, yet profound, irony. For it was not only because of the drought that "there was no water, and everything was dead," but, symbolically, because the schemes and theories themselves were arid. It is only when Jarvis and Kumalo meet humbly as two human beings, each aware of the weight of the other's suffering, and therefore of their common humanity, that the drought breaks and the rain comes at last to the valley of Ndotsheni.

Paton's *Cry, the Beloved Country* offers no blueprint for society. What it does objectify is individual recognition of personal responsibility. Such recognition depends on a process of self-discovery, a process which both James Jarvis and Stephen Kumalo endure in the novel. The effect of this artistic method on the reader may be analogous to the effect Hamlet intended his play to have on his uncle, King Claudius, when he said: "The play's the thing wherein I'll catch the conscience of the King." Ideally, the reader of *Cry, the Beloved Country* undergoes a process of self-discovery, too; having observed James Jarvis suffer the deepest and most intense experience of his life, one may come to understand the significance of Jarvis' later actions towards Ndotsheni as expressions of a newly recognized moral responsibility.

The crucial development in the characters of both Jarvis and Kumalo is that each comes to recognize how individual fear or indifference infects society with moral paralysis; and that the antidote for this paralysis is individual courage willing to go forward in faith. They do not wait, therefore, for some miraculous healing of this paralysis to be brought about by the direct intervention of God, or through the implementation of some scheme for a final solution, or through the flowering of the promises of some manifesto. They act by taking whatever steps are possible to them as individuals in the immediate present. A road taken in faith has no certainty of arrival; if it did, faith would be unnecessary. *Cry, the Beloved Country,* therefore, rightly concludes with an acceptance of uncertainty, and not with a blueprint for the future: "But when the dawn will come of our emancipation, from the fear of bondage and the bondage of fear, why, that is a secret." (277)

CHAPTER 4

The Pride of Pure Race:
Too Late the Phalarope

I *The Sin Against the Race*

PATON'S second novel, *Too Late the Phalarope*, is similar in certain respects to *Cry, the Beloved Country*, but, for the most part, the novels differ strikingly. Both works have similarities of style and dramatic method, and each relates a comparatively simple story. *Too Late the Phalarope* tells the story of Pieter van Vlaanderen, a young police lieutenant decorated in war and also nationally famous as a football player. He is a married man with two children, highly respected in the rural Afrikaner community and, indeed, the kind of man in whose presence other men feel constrained to subdue loud talk or off-color jokes. Yet Pieter van Vlaanderen transgresses the strict prohibitions of the South African Immorality Act which forbids sexual relations between members of different races, and thereby brings tragic destruction on himself and his family.

But the differences between the two novels are more significant than the similarities. *Too Late the Phalarope* concentrates on the inner struggles in the soul of one man in the South African social situation; for the clamor of many voices and the broad overview, it substitutes an inner dialogue between two aspects of a divided personality. Furthermore, while the theme of restoration is still fundamental in the second novel, it is approached indirectly, and its attendant note of hope is muted. This is due in part to its literary method, which resembles the method of Greek tragedy more closely than does that of the earlier novel, but it also may be due to the changes that meanwhile took place in South Africa's political climate.

The note of hope in *Cry, the Beloved Country* had some real basis in fact. There were signs in the months immediately following World War II that South African society was prepared to accept progressive change in relations among the races. In 1946 Prime Minister J. C. Smuts had appointed a commission to look into South Africa's urban conditions and the problems of migratory African labor—the very conditions and problems that impelled Paton to write *Cry, the Beloved Country.* It was generally expected that this commission, known as the Fagan Commission, would present liberal recommendations to Parliament. It was also generally anticipated that any such recommendations would be implemented by Parliament through the influence of the Deputy Prime Minister Jan Hofmeyr, who then seemed likely to succeed General Smuts as Prime Minister.

In 1948, the same year that *Cry, the Beloved Country* appeared, the typical rhythm of South African politics reasserted itself, for any suspicion that the Liberal Spirit is working among parliamentary leaders starts a ground-swell for racial intolerance among the white voters, particularly in rural areas. And in the general elections of that year, Dr. Malan's Nationalist Party received an unexpectedly large plurality for its policy of *apartheid.* This policy denies Africans the right to permanent residence in the towns, and emphasizes ineradicable cultural differences between their tribal heritage and the heritage of "Western Civilization," which is thought to be the birthright of whites only. Jan Hofmeyr died a few months after this election, and with him went much of the hope of powerful, outspoken opposition to the new government's policies. In these respects at least, the hope of going forward in faith implicitly present in *Cry, the Beloved Country* was diminished.

By 1952, the year that Paton wrote *Too Late the Phalarope* during a three-month period in London and in an English seaside boarding house, the new Nationalist government in South Africa had begun implementing its policies of *apartheid* with little regard for opposition views. Paton did not, however, turn his new novel into an attack on *apartheid,* nor into propaganda for any political cause. His choice of the magnanimous Afrikaner woman Tante Sophie as the narrator proves to be a valuable device in this respect. He does not even set the novel with any obviousness in the post-1948 period, and he ignores the immediate social and economic manifestations of *apartheid.* Instead he probes penetratingly into its roots in the ideal of Pure Race; and makes manifest the extent to which this ideal—placed above all other considerations—constitutes a false deity, or "heretical Christianity," as he calls it elsewhere. It is this pride in Pure Race, set up as an ideal, that the narrator, Tante Sophie, has in mind in her summing up: "I pray we shall not walk arrogant, remembering Herod whom an Angel of the Lord struck down, for that he made himself a God." (272) Sophie's view implies that this racial arrogance has affinities with the Greek concept of *hybris*—the special manifestation of pride that incurs tragic retribution. *Hybris* is the arrogation by men of attributes proper only to the gods, and tragedy is the inevitable destruction meted out to *hybris*.

Too Late the Phalarope is a Greek tragedy in modern South African dress. It is set in a small town in the eastern Transvaal—a district populated almost wholly by Afrikaans-speaking white farmers who cherish the four fundamental and inseparable tenets of Afrikaner Nationalism: *Volk, Kerk, Taal, Land*. The *Volk* is the separate and unique Afrikaner People descended from the Voortrekkers; the *Kerk* is the Afrikaner branch of the Dutch Reformed Church to which, ideally, all the *Volk* adhere; the *Taal* is the Afrikaans language which, in place of a national boundary, identifies their nationhood; and the *Land* is the soil of South Africa, sacred to the Afrikaner *Volk* in almost the same sense that the Promised Land was sacred to the Israelites.

These fundamental ideals are summed up in the novel by the Afrikaner patriarch, old Jakob van Vlaanderen, when he rebukes the besotted Flip van Vuuren who persisted in demanding, "what's the point of living, what's the point of life?": "So Jakob van Vlaanderen stood up from his chair, and said in a voice of thunder, the point of living is to serve the Lord your God, and to uphold the honour of your church and language and people, take him home." (92) Jakob van Vlaanderen represents the attitude of those Afrikaans-speaking South Africans who refused to accept Louis Botha's ideal of bringing all white South Africans together in a common patriotism. His wife and his sister, Tante Sophie, adhere to Louis Botha's ideal discussed in Chapter 1, above; his son Pieter, in the finer aspects of his character, might be said to personify Botha's ideal.

This difference in their estimates of where the duties of patriotism lie constitutes one of the causes of friction between Jakob and his son Pieter. At the outbreak of World War II, the South African Parliament was divided on the question of entering the

war against Hitler's Germany on Britain's side, or remaining neutral, and General Smuts carried his motion for participation by a
very narrow majority. The people were similarly divided. So it
was found expedient to agree that men already in the armed
forces and police should be permitted either to retain their posi-
tions at home or to volunteer for service abroad. Those who so
volunteered were identified by orange tabs on their shoulder-
straps, which, unfortunately, sharply distinguished them from
those who did not; the oath taken by these volunteers came to be
known as "the red oath" from the color of the tabs. Jakob van
Vlaanderen was one of those who saw the war as "an English
war" in which no true Afrikaner should participate: "And when
his son Pieter took the red oath and had gone to war, he would
bear no mention of his name . . ." When Pieter returned, Jakob
would refer to his service medals and decorations, which included
the Distinguished Service Order, as "foreign trash."

Pieter's volunteering for war service was later to play a large
part in his tragic downfall. Since he had attained the rank of
major in the army, he returned to the local police force as an
officer. He therefore outranked Sergeant Steyn, who had longer
service, but who, agreeing with Jakob's Afrikaner patriotism, had
refused to take "the red oath." This is the source of the enmity
that makes Sergeant Steyn the instrument of Pieter's destruction.
Steyn is something of an Iago, but his hatred is not motiveless.

This general climate of nationalism lying behind the conflicts of
Too Late the Phalarope is one of the elements that makes it an
authentic portrait of an important segment of South African life.
As he did in Cry, the Beloved Country, Paton adds to this general
authenticity by weaving certain actual events of the time into the
action of his plot. In his hands these actual events become dramatic properties inseparable from the action of the story.

One of these "properties" is the book that Lieutenant Pieter van
Vlaanderen gives as a birthday gift to his father. The non-fictional
model for this fictional book was The Birds of South Africa—a
comprehensive work with fine color illustrations like the Audubon
series in the United States, published in South Africa in 1948.[1]
For Paton, one of whose hobbies is birdwatching, this would
have been a memorable event, made even more memorable by
the fact that its author, the respected naturalist Austin Roberts,
died that year. The title of this book pleases old Jakob van Vlaan-

deren, to whose intense nationalism the name South Africa borders on the sacred, but the name of the author repels him. He will not even mention it, and he always refers to the author as "the Englishman." Since Paton does not reveal the author's name, readers are left to assume that old Jakob's repugnance is a measure of his hostility to Englishmen in general. But there would be good reason for Jakob's special repugnance toward the name Roberts, for the British general whose armies invaded the Transvaal across the very terrain of the novel's setting, and who for a time during the Boer War virtually ruled South Africa, was General Lord Roberts.

It may be the touch of obscurity resulting from Paton's reluctance to extend to his readers a clearer motive for Jakob's repugnance that leads some to seek symbolic significance in the book of birds and, in particular, in the elusive little bird, the phalarope. The book of birds does affect the relations between Jakob and his son, but it is not a symbol in any exact sense. Neither is the phalarope a symbol. It is an actual bird about whose habits old Jakob, in fact, knew more than "the Englishman" who wrote the book. In *The Birds of South Africa,* Austin Roberts has some hesitation in classifying the phalarope as a South African bird, because he has only one recorded observation of each of the two species of phalarope, the "Grey" and the "Red-necked," on South African coasts. Jakob knew the phalarope as a fairly common inland bird also, and the Englishman's ignorance was a topic, therefore, that he was happy to discuss even with his son Pieter, with whom he had never before achieved rapport.

Another actual event of the period—or an account closely based on it—helps Paton to establish the atmosphere of obsession with racial purity in a society where the most unforgivable thing is to break "the iron law that no white man might touch a black woman"; and that the most terrible thing in the world is to have such a transgression discovered. This is the case of "the man Smith," modeled on an actual contemporary case of a white farmer who murdered an African servant girl who was pregnant by him. In the hope of preventing the discovery of his victim's identity, which might lead to his own discovery, "the man Smith," with his wife's complicity, cut off and hid the murdered girl's head. In Paton's account, this gruesome crime by an otherwise mild-mannered man is interpreted principally as a consequence

72   ALAN PATON

of his fear that his illicit sexual relations across the racial line
would be discovered.

This account of "the man Smith" provides a dramatic instance
of the general air of intense concern with the issue of race-mixture
that followed the Nationalist Party election victory of 1948. There
was then a law in force against illicit sexual relations between
white and non-white. This was Act 5 of 1927, under which Lieutenant Pieter van Vlaanderen is charged in the novel *Too Late the
Phalarope*. In 1949 and 1950 there were further extensions of this
basic law: the Prohibition of Mixed Marriages Act of 1949, and
the Immorality Act Amendment Act of 1950. The basic law may
at one time have had the merit claimed for it of protecting African
women from the whims of white overlords, but the extensions of
the basic Act reveal the essence of the new Nationalist ideal. By
prohibiting interracial marriage even at a church ceremony, and
by extending the Act to cover any racial mixing, as for example,
between Indian and Cape Colored communities, the emphasis is
clearly focused on the ideal of Pure Race, and not on justifiable
protection of vulnerable women. One may find interesting corroboration of this attitude in textbooks widely used in Transvaal
schools. In the chapter "Race Relations: White and non-White" in
one junior high school textbook in social studies, there is a sub-
heading "The Sin of Race Mixture" which argues that God wills
separate races. This account culminates in a long quotation from
someone identified only as "one of our great statesmen," that begins with what is tantamount to a summary of *Too Late the
Phalarope:* "We must all keep our people white. Great is the pain
for blood-relatives and friends if anyone sins against this highest
law; greater still is the scandal when a people sins against its own
blood." [2]

It is in this context of an ideal of racial purity that classified
race-mixture as the ultimate sin—the sin "against this highest law"
as the textbook puts it—that Paton sets the tragedy of Pieter van
Vlaanderen.

Finally, one should recall in this connection Paton's own account of the times in the Public Affairs pamphlet *South Africa
Today*. This pamphlet, intended for American audiences unfamiliar with the complexities of race relations in South Africa, is a
scrupulously fair appraisal of the trend of events in South Africa
in 1951—a year or so before he set to work on *Too Late the Phala-*

rope. As a contemporary account, *South Africa Today* provides a very useful background to Paton's novels. It gives a brief historical sketch of the origins and development of South Africa's racial groups, and indicates the current status of each. Its account of "Modern Industry and Tribal Life" with a subsection on "Crime and Disintegration" gives, in small space, the social record dramatized in *Cry, the Beloved Country.* Its account of "The Immediate Situation," more relevant to *Too Late the Phalarope,* points out that racial separation was not a new concept introduced by the Nationalist Party. What was new was the strengthening of the framework of laws requiring the compliance of all with the ideals of *apartheid.* At this early stage, much of this framework of laws was still only 'projected,' but among those already passed into law, Paton notes: "The present Government has amended and widened the Immorality Act of the Hertzog Government . . . It has passed a Mixed Marriages Act which now forbids marriages between whites and non-whites."

Paton makes one statement in *South Africa Today* about his own attitude to Afrikaner nationalism that has a significant bearing on the tone of *Too Late the Phalarope,* and of his other works, particularly the biography of Jan Hofmeyr. He concludes *South Africa Today* at the point where he feels he has written enough for his readers to grasp "the complexity and tragedy" of South Africa's situation, saying:

This situation is more tragic for the Afrikaner Nationalist than for the English-speaking South African, for although both know no other home, this is true in a different sense of the Afrikaner. In this I feel for him painfully and deeply. That is why, for example, I never use hurtful language in giving any account of Nationalist policies. But the world will take no account of his fierce devotion . . . nor of my compassion.

It is this attitude, including its compassion, that Tante Sophie brings to *Too Late the Phalarope,* and to that extent her fictional character incorporates something of Paton himself.

Various characters in *Too Late the Phalarope* embody contrasting attitudes to this sin against the highest law. Some, representing a majority view in the town of Venterspan, uphold the law with iron determination. These include Pieter's father, old Jakob van Vlaanderen, and his father-in-law, who declares he would

shoot the offender like a dog. The proponents of this kind of justice include also his fellow policeman, Sergeant Steyn, and the
previously admiring young recruit, Vorster. Others view Pieter's
transgression with greater compassion. But these are a minority,
represented by his aunt, Tante Sophie; his mother; the English-
speaking police officer, Captain Massingham; and the Jewish
storekeeper, Matthew Kaplan, who is affectionately known by the
Afrikaans diminutive, "Kappie." It is chiefly through the contrasting attitudes of old Jakob and Tante Sophie that we see the opposing themes of destruction and restoration brought into confrontation; and here the sacrificial justice demanded by the iron
law outweighs the compassionate justice exhorted by Christ to his
followers. Ironically, this victory of vengeance over compassion is
exactly what the novel propounds as the greatest of all offenses
from a Christian standpoint. Pieter's superior officer, Captain
Massingham, sums this up when he says: "An offender must be
punished, *mejuffrou,* I don't argue about that. But to punish and
not to restore, that is the greatest of all offences." And Tante
Sophie, significantly, responds, "Is that the sin against the Holy
Ghost?" (292)

These contrasting attitudes, pitting what amounts to the acceptance of inexorable fate against the impulse toward forgiveness and restoration, bear significantly on the status of *Too Late
the Phalarope* as a tragedy in the literary sense. It may, therefore,
be useful to look more closely at Jakob and Sophie, the two chief
embodiments of these attitudes.

II *Judgment or Mercy*

Jakob van Vlaanderen, as his name suggests, combines some of
the qualities of an Old Testament patriarch with the Afrikaner's
elemental Flemish roots. Enshrined in his Transvaal home is the
great family Bible in the Dutch language version, containing the
names of the van Vlaanderens for 150 years. His forebears had
brought it with them from the Cape Colony when they trekked
inland to set up their independent Boer republics beyond the
reach of British laws and their equal application to white and
black. Jakob van Vlaanderen was a strong-willed giant of a man
who understood the word obedience "better than he understood
the word love." He was an upright man, just in accordance with
his own unwavering principles. He believed that his duty to God

demanded that he uphold the separateness and racial purity of the Afrikaner people. As befitted his exclusive nationalism, he was a lover of all things South African, including the birds of the veld.

Jakob understood strength and determination in a man, but not sensitivity; he treated the sensitive side of his son's character—his pleasure in such fragile beautiful things as flowers and stamps—with harshness and suspicion. Eventually, prompted by his son's gift of a book of South African birds, he took hesitant steps toward reconciliation. He arranged to show Pieter the phalarope, the little wading bird about whose habits the author of the book was mistaken; and, although perplexed by the whole thing, he even purchased some expensive stamps for him.

This thaw in the iciness of his attitude toward his son adds great poignancy to the novel by suggesting what might have been; but it is not the fact that father and son recognized a common interest too late that supplies the essential element of tragedy. An essential element of tragedy, in addition to the flaw in the hero's character, is that the fate of those enmeshed in its web is determined, like that of King Oedipus, by a power outside their control. This external determining element is present in *Too Late the Phalarope* as a form of historical determinism attendant upon the fundamental assumption that the Afrikaner people are a Pure Race set apart. Therefore, when Jakob hears that his son has "sinned against the race," he knows exactly what his duty to the race demands of him: "So he took the pen and ink, and he crossed out the name of Pieter van Vlaanderen from the book . . ." Then, referring to Pieter's gift of the book of birds: "You will take the book, he said, and the pipe, and everything that the man ever gave to me, and every likeness of him, and everything in this house that has anything to do with him, and you will burn and destroy them all." (251) This ritual of denial culminates in prayer to God for the destruction of his son's soul; for Jakob solemnly opened the family Bible and read "the most terrible words that man has ever written" from the Hundred and Ninth Psalm, beginning: *"When he shall be judged, let him be condemned; and let his prayer become sin."* And old Jakob read on, blind to the irony that "the most terrible words" of the Psalm are explicitly directed against the man who *"who remembered not to show mercy."*

Old Jakob's actions are predictable. The reader, in fact, accepts them as the inevitable expression of his character. But they are ultimately dictated by an impersonal force outside himself rather than by a father's response to a son's transgression. For Old Jakob could not act otherwise and still maintain the purity of race as the highest law.

The contrasting qualities of mercy and compassion are embodied in Jakob's maiden sister, Tante Sophie van Vlaanderen, who relates Pieter's story. Sophie is a watcher set apart from normal family life and love by a severe facial disfigurement. She has lived all her life in Jakob's house, and she has lavished on her young nephew, Pieter, all the affection of her own unfulfilled maternal instincts. We therefore see both father and son from her sympathetic viewpoint. Her concern for these men, and indeed for all men, is deeply Christian; her Christianity, based on love, contrasts strikingly with Jakob's narrower, puritanical Christianity that respects obedience above all. As narrator, Sophie presents the other characters in all their human frailty; but she refrains from passing judgment on them. She is at pains, for example, to show the human side of Jakob: "For some said he was a hard and loveless man, and would ride down any that stood in his way without pity or mercy. But I tell you it was not true." Yet she is not a party to Jakob's extreme devotion to exclusive Afrikaner nationalism; she prefers to retain her allegiance to Louis Botha's policy of reconciliation.

Sophie has other advantages as a narrator besides her magnanimity of outlook. Having lived all her life with the van Vlaanderen family, she can link her knowledge of Pieter's childhood relations with his father to the events of his tragedy. She recognizes that his downfall is not brought about wholly by momentary temptation, but that it is a consequence of accumulated life experience. Her ability to reveal how past events foreshadowed destruction intensifies the element of tragic inevitability in the novel.

Although Sophie is an observer set aside, with little power over events, she is emotionally involved in the fortunes of Pieter and Jakob. This appears to be one of Paton's main motives in creating her. Speaking of the vitality of the South African novel in English, particularly in the hands of writers of English or Jewish extraction, or Colored writers like Peter Abrahams, Paton has remarked that in South Africa, where the racial struggle primarily pits African against Afrikaner: "It is the Englishman, the Jew and the

Coloured man, who are, even when they are drawn into the struggle, the observers. It is they who are better placed than either
Afrikaner or African . . . to see the real drama that history has
unfolded, even when they are deeply or emotionally involved." [3]

In *Too Late the Phalarope,* Tante Sophie fills an analogous role.
She is presented to us as being clearly aware of her own powers of
observation. She knows that she developed these powers because
she was set apart from the ordinary stream of life by her disfigurement: "I have learned to know the meaning of unnoticed things,
of a pulse that beats suddenly, of a glance that moves from here
to there . . ." It was she who rightly suspected the marital difficulties between Pieter and his wife Nella; it was she who correctly
interpreted Stephanie's sensual invitation to Pieter; it was she who
felt uncomfortable about the flirtatious Cousin Anna, who wore
the yellow trousers. Paton's device of the secret diary as one
source of her information may be an arbitrary one, but it proves
useful in establishing her reliability as an observer; for, at key
points, she is able to quote from the diary to confirm her original
intuition. [4]

Whatever her technical limitations, one must admit that only a
narrator of Tante Sophie's qualities of mind could provide a suitable vehicle for the religious theme of the novel: namely, that it is
not the judgment of God but the judgment of men that is a
stranger to compassion.

III *Temptation and Tragedy*

As has already been remarked, *Too Late the Phalarope* resembles *Cry, the Beloved Country* in certain aspects of its artistic
method. It is similarly arranged in dramatic sequences depending
largely on effective dialogue and the support of a modified chorus.
Furthermore its plot has a similar double action. The plot of *Too
Late the Phalarope* is divided almost exactly into two complementary movements. The first gradually unfolds the events leading to
Pieter van Vlaanderen's temptation and sin; the second reveals
him enmeshed in a web of tragedy and destruction. Chapters 1
through 19 may be said, therefore, to comprise The Book of
Temptation; Chapters 20 through 39, The Book of Retribution.
The two complementary actions of the plot imply an ironic contrast; namely, that even though Pieter's adultery transgresses the

laws of God, it is not God, but an idol—the false deity of Pure Race—that exacts the terrible retribution of Pieter's destruction, and the destruction of all belonging to him.

It should perhaps be noted, too, that just as *Cry, the Beloved Country* superimposes a religious theme on a primarily social one, *Too Late the Phalarope* superimposes a religious theme on a psychological one. Both novels may therefore be read on more than one level.

In what is here termed The Book of Temptation, Paton represents Pieter van Vlaanderen's temptation and sin as a consequence of several interrelated causes, no one of which is singled out as dominating him so completely that he cannot resist it. Ultimately, he deliberately chooses to seek out the black girl Stephanie; without this element of deliberate choice there would be no intentional offending against the laws of God, and therefore no sin in the Christian sense. The web of contributive causes includes elements that we may tentatively distinguish as psychological, spiritual, physical, and instinctive.

One psychological cause of Pieter's transgression is deeply rooted in the duality of his own nature. He is aware of two conflicting sides to his character: the one, brave and upright; the other possessed by an elemental urge attracting him, he says, to what he most hated. He conceals this side of his character behind a mask of cold reserve, and when this urge takes hold of him he calls it "the mad sickness." Evidently this "mad sickness" is a strong, but unwanted, sexual attraction to women outside his marriage. His comment on his father's simple, matter-of-fact statemen that he had never touched a woman other than his wife is: "I felt . . . a feeling of envy too, and wonder that I was otherwise." Since Pieter also envies those fellow students at the university who spoke of their physical revulsion to the touch of a nonwhite person—a revulsion he does not share—it seems clear that by "the mad sickness" he means a sexual desire forbidden by the iron law of his people "that no black woman should be touched by a white man."

The novel suggests that the psychological conflict in Pieter's character has roots in his childhood relations with his father. Pieter, referring to his father's anger at his interest in stamp collecting, says bitterly to Matthew Kaplan: "There was trouble long before the stamps . . . I was born before the stamps." In this respect Pieter's desire for Stephanie can be explained as a psycho-logical impulse to revolt against all his father stood for. But Paton does not rationalize Pieter's action to the extent of lifting the bur-den of responsibility from his shoulders and transferring it to old Jakob. Pieter was conscious of his problem, and could have sought help. Indeed, his successive attempts to reveal himself to the young clergyman, Dominee Vos, to Kappie, and to Captain Mas-singham, constitute one link between the theme of temptation, which he can choose to resist, and the web of tragedy manipu-lated by forces outside his power. There is tragic irony in his suc-cessive failures to unburden himself; on each occasion that he at-tempts to do so, the regard in which others hold him—their wor-shipful attitude towards him as their hero—intervenes. Even though he had but one thought in his mind—"to tell one human soul of the misery of my life, that I was tempted by what I hated" —a fatal flaw prevents him from doing so; and he asks, but leaves unanswered, "Was it pride that prevented me?"

Another source of Pieter's psychological conflict is the tension between him and his wife Nella, arising from her attitude to mar-ried love. However, it would be more relevant to Paton's wider purpose, embracing the problem of love at several levels, to note the possibility of spiritual, in addition to psychological, roots for Nella's attitude. In her marriage, Sophie tells us, Nella had "some idea that was good and true but twisted in some small place, that the love of the body, though good and true, was apart from the love of the soul." In so describing Nella, Paton seems to be point-ing beyond such commonplace categories as prudery or Puritan-ism, to the classic Christian heresies of the Manicheans and the Gnostics. The extreme Manichean doctrine holds that man's body is the work of the Devil and that the soul is engaged in eternal war with it; it is akin to the Gnostic rejection of man's material nature in favor of an idealized abstraction comparable, for exam-ple, to the concept of Pure Race. Nella's attitude to married love may be, partly, a heritage from the religious Puritanism of her people; but her extreme revulsion at hearing that the boy Dick had attempted to accost the black girl, Stephanie, suggests that her other heritage, the ideal of Pure Race, is inextricably entwined with her religious outlook. Since Paton has elsewhere referred to the ideal of Pure Race as "a Christian heresy," Nella's attitude may well embody the view that the racial ideals enshrined in the

theories of Pure Race constitute a modern Manichean or Gnostic
outlook. The point need not be insisted upon, but it provides, like
Book Three of *Cry, the Beloved Country,* another instance of
Paton's distrust of abstract utopian, or totalitarian, schemes that
substitute an inhuman perfection for the flesh and blood realities
of the human condition.

If Nella's part in Pieter's susceptibility to temptation is remote,
the part played by Anna is immediate and physical. Anna occupies Tante Sophie's thoughts to a surprising extent—wholly out of
proportion to her two brief appearances in the novel. Anna, who
is described as "a kind of cousin," works in the city and has ac-
quired city attitudes towards fashions in dress and social drinking.
She says openly that Pieter was the only man she ever wanted to
marry. When Sophie reveals her dislike of those city women who
wear trousers of various colors, she dwells on the point that "it is
the yellow trousers that anger me most of all." Later, she tells us
that Anna "smokes and wears the yellow trousers that I most dislike." Not really wicked, Anna is flashy, bored by the small town,
and slightly vulgar. She is, ultimately, the temptress who, partly
unwittingly, is the immediate instrument of Pieter's destruction.
At the critical psychological moment when his black mood is
deepest as a consequence of Nella's obtuse letter, Sergeant Steyn's
mistake, and the high emotional temperature that caused him to
write his letter of resignation, Anna waylays him with feminine
wiles and the plea "I'm dying for a drink." So, in the Royal Hotel,
they have brandy after brandy, "more than he had every drunk
before." Aroused by the brandies, Anna's company, and her part-
ing kiss, he goes to meet Stephanie in the vacant ground. Paton
implies, nevertheless, that Pieter's choice is deliberate; for whatever forces the underlying psychological drives, the brandies, and
Anna's company may have released, his final preparations for the
encounter with Stephanie are calculated.

In contrast to Pieter's agonized struggles to avoid temptation,
the black girl Stephanie has a simple, uncomplicated purpose for
seeking him out. Her life in and out of prison, where she has been
sent for brewing illicit liquor, is devoted to the single-minded aim
of retaining her sole possesson—her illegitimate child. In her instinctive preoccupation with the safety of her child, she seizes on
the only possibility she can think of for recruiting this great man's
protection; it is for the same reason—to avert danger to her child

—that she later carries out Sergeant Steyn's plan to destroy him.

The second movement of the plot of *Too Late the Phalarope,* The Book of Retribution, reaches beyond the interesting psychological and moral aspects of temptation toward the pity and terror of tragedy. The opening episodes of this second movement parallel those opening chapters of the first movement that establish the social atmosphere in which transgressing the prohibitions of the Immorality Act constitutes the most terrible thing in the world. In this case Paton skillfully intensifies the atmosphere, and involves the reader's emotions in the pity and terror that Aristotle identifies as the characteristic effect of tragedy. Pity draws out our sympathy for the tragic character so that we share in his dread of impending evil; terror, in Aristotle's view, is the powerful sense of the utter destructiveness of the impending evil.

First, however, we should note the simple ease with which Paton solves a literary problem that many critics have declared to be insurmountable: the problem of reconciling a Christian viewpoint with tragedy as a literary form. These critics argue on various grounds. One ground is that the Christian conception of free will cannot admit of determined, inescapable fate. Another is that Christianity can admit only one possible form of tragedy, namely, damnation. Paton undercuts the dilemma by building his tragedy, not on the consequences of Pieter van Vlaanderen's act understood as a sin against God (he leaves this as an inner, private matter), but on the consequences of his act understood as a "sin against the race."

Paton therefore disposes of the sin against God's law in a single paragraph, in which Pieter prays to God in Heaven, partly for forgiveness for his act, and partly for forgiveness for presuming to pray at such a moment. This short paragraph closes with a striking metaphor for the theological assertion that sin cuts man off from God's love:

For he had a vision that a trumpet had been blown in Heaven, and that the Lord Most High had ordered the closing of the doors, that no prayer might enter in from such a man, who knowing the laws and the Commandments, had, of his own choice and will, defied them. (154)

From this point on, Paton's literary concern is not with Pieter's guilt, but with his terror of discovery. For even while Pieter was praying he heard a twig crack, and he suspected a watcher in the dark. Thereafter he prays repeatedly, not for forgiveness, but that he might not be discovered: "but now it was another mercy that he sought, not to be saved from sin but from its consequences." In the first movement of the plot we encountered "the man Smith" driven by the same terror to a desperate act. But whereas Smith's terror is merely implied, Paton builds up Pieter's mounting terror in great detail, and skillfully involves the reader. After an account of Pieter's ritual cleansing of himself in Chapter 20, Paton devotes four chapters to his three days of terror. Chapters 21 and 22 concern the first day of terror. Chapter 23 begins: "The second day of terror was as bad as the first . . ."; Chapter 24 begins: "And the third day of terror was the worst. . . ." The significance of these episodes goes beyond their immediate value as instruments of suspense; for only by demonstrating the intensity of the tragic character's terror of the impending evil, can Paton assure the reader that the tragic blow, when it comes, is tantamount to total annihilation.

But the blow does not fall on Pieter immediately, and for a time he feels assured that his prayers to avoid discovery have been answered. Therefore when the blow does fall, it comes suddenly and from an unexpected quarter. The events he interpreted as signs that his transgression had been discovered turn out to be mere coincidence or the shallow practical jokes of the welfare worker, Japie Grobler. Pieter's endurance of terror brings a full recognition that the consequences of his act, if discovered, will involve not only himself but Nella and his children and all who bore the name van Vlaanderen. There is hope that his determination to avoid bringing destruction on them will strengthen him against the desire for Stephanie.

These glimmerings of hope seem to point toward a new dawn when old Jakob arranges the family picnic where he and Pieter watch for the phalarope together. Their discovery of a shared interest opens a breach in the wall of hostility between them. If it was this hostility that nourished the psychological roots of Pieter's compulsion to rebel against the iron laws his father represents, the discovery of a common interest in the phalarope could imply that unconscious motivation would no longer drive Pieter into the arms of Stephanie.

But the growing inner determination, the picnic, and the phala-

rope come too late. Sergeant Steyn, like Iago in his enmity, takes a
hint of suspicion for surety. He sets a trap for Pieter, and Stephanie, out of fear for the security of her child, carries out Steyn's
purpose. She plants the evidence on Pieter and turns witness
against him, and he is convicted and sentenced to prison for con-
travening the Immorality Act, No. 5 of 1927.

Pieter's destruction as a public man is more complete and enduring than his prison sentence. As he had once explained to
young Dick: "It's a thing that's never forgiven, never forgotten.
The court may give you a year, two years. But outside it's a sentence for life." In the society that made the iron laws there is no
hope of public forgiveness or restoration. The characters representing the forces of arrogant pride in race treat the transgressor
with supreme contempt. Therefore, in *Too Late the Phalarope,* as
in *Cry, the Beloved Country,* the theme of restoration centers
around the acceptance of personal responsibility by those who,
while detesting the sin, continue to love the sinner and forgive
him. These characters, representing the forces of love, try in their
various ways to restore Pieter. His friend Kappie, the Jewish
storekeeper, suffers mutely with him, but acts with courage to dis-
suade him from suicide. Captain Massingham is able to put the
theme of restoration into words. It is he who recognizes that to
destroy and not to restore is the greatest of all offenses, and it is
his words that make Sophie understand that Pieter's future rests
with Nella, the injured wife: "There is a hard law, *mejouffrou,*
that when a deep injury is done to us we never recover until we
forgive." (266) The most meaningful forgiveness must come from
Nella, for she is the person most wronged by Pieter's action.

As Sergeant Steyn's hatred was an agent of Pieter's destruction,
his mother's love is the agent of the measure of restoration possible
to him. Sophie attributes Nella's return to stand by Pieter during
his trial to the agency of his mother's love: "the girl came back,
silent but steadfast, borne on the strong deep river of the mother's
love." The love personified by Pieter's mother contrasts with the
intense self-concern underlying total devotion of others to pride in
Pure Race. We learn little of her in the novel beyond Sophie's
estimate that "if ever a woman was all love, it was she. . . ." (4)
Her unselfish love is set as a healing spring in the desert of de-
structive racial pride. Significantly, in her personal relations with
people and her humanitarian concern for the welfare of others,

she shares the characteristic unselfishness of Arthur Jarvis in *Cry, the Beloved Country.* Thus she provides another fictional parallel for the qualities of Edith Rheinallt Jones that Paton describes in "A Deep Experience." Sophie's final summing up suggests this when she says that Pieter's story would be better told by her sister: "And I wish she could have written it, for maybe of the power of her love that never sought itself, men would have turned to the holy task of pardon, that the body of the Lord might not be wounded twice, and virtue come of our offences." (272)

CHAPTER 5

Tales from a Troubled Land

I *The Short Stories*

PATON'S involvement in the newly founded Liberal Party, which he was to lead as National Chairman (and later as National President) from 1956 on, drew him increasingly into South African public affairs during the decade of the 1950's. Since he finds it necessary to withdraw completely from all other activities when engaged on a book, he again had to choose between the possibility of artistic creation and the necessity for constructive social action. Paton produced no major work between *Too Late the Phalarope* in 1953 and his great biography of Jan Hofmeyr in 1964. He continued to write short fiction, poetry, and drama, but much of his writing during this decade was occasioned by the political and religious implications of South Africa's racial ideologies.

A collection of his short fiction was published in 1961 under the variant titles, *Tales from a Troubled Land* in the United States, and *Debbie Go Home* in Britian.[1] Most of the ten stories in this collection had appeared in South African magazines beginning with "The Worst Thing in His Life" in 1951. Three of them appeared for the first time in this collection. Six of these ten stories are set in Diepkloof Reformatory, and three of these six were later developed into the play *Sponono* by Paton and Krishna Shah. The four stories that have their settings outside the reformatory walls more closely share the profound depth of vision and universal appeal of his novels than the reformatory stories do; however, the implications of these latter stories are by no means confined to the particulars of Diepkloof.

II *The Kafkaesque World of the Cape Colored People*

Of the four stories in *Tales from a Troubled Land* set outside the reformatory walls, at least one, "The Waste Land," is a miniature masterpiece in the art of short fiction. Two others, that treat a

South African racial group not hitherto encountered in Paton's fiction, have qualities that resemble the best aspects of his novels. These two stories, "A Life for a Life" and "Debbie Go Home," look as perceptively into the human condition of South Africa's Colored people (that is, the racial group composed of people of mixed blood) as *Cry, the Beloved Country* does into the plight of the Africans, and *Too Late the Phalarope* into the agony of the Afrikaners.

"Debbie Go Home," the title story of the British edition, recounts a domestic conflict among the members of a Colored family. The father, Jim de Villiers, returns home early from his place of employment with the knowledge that the government's new Industrial Conciliation Act, popularly known as the Job Reservation Act, can turn him out of work by reserving for whites only the occupation he has followed for years. His early return surprises his wife and teenage daughter as they are preparing a new gown for the girl to wear to the Debutantes Ball for Colored Girls, which is to be held at City Hall in the presence of a high government official—the white Administrator of the Province.

Jim de Villiers angrily forbids the gown and the Ball. His son Johnny, who belongs to a militant student organization at the University, supports him. Indeed, the son and other members of the student Unity Movement plan to picket the Debutantes Ball, and have already prepared signs and placards for the picket line bearing such slogans as "Welcome, spick little lickspittle" and "Debbie Go Home"—a local twist on "Yankee Go Home."

The story that unfolds from the domestic crisis of the de Villiers family revolves about the mother's determination to obtain for her daughter at least "one night, in a nice dress and the coloured lights, dancing before the Administrator in the City Hall"; and how she enlists the aid of her cynical, militant son to achieve her aim. But in the process we become aware of an unbridgeable gulf between the hopes and outlooks of the older and younger generations of the Colored people.

In this respect "Debbie Go Home" has an important place in the canon of Paton's writings on South Africa, one equalled only by the two novels. For if *Cry, the Beloved Country* embodies the most significant aspects of South Africa's social record in the 1940's, and *Too Late the Phalarope* embodies the intense preoccupation with Pure Race that marked the opening of the 1950's,

"Debbie Go Home" points to ominous signs in the social record of the 1960's—a crucial turn in the traditional relationships among the races.

In "Debbie Go Home," Jim de Villiers returns from work with news of a new law: "It says the Minister can reserve any occupation. So we may have to go. We, we. The Coloured men." In his anger and frustration he curses the government and its representative, the Administrator, for this and for the other legal cornerstones of *apartheid*, such as the law removing Colored voters from the common roll, the Group Areas Act that determines their place of residence, and the Population Registration Act that determines everyone's racial classification. As de Villiers puts it: ". . . a law that took away my job, and a law that took away my vote, and a law that's going to take away my house, all because I've a coloured skin." (T. 83, D. 16)

But in spite of Jim de Villiers' anger at the spate of *apartheid* legislation, his son Johnny accurately perceives a deeper cause for his frustration than the specific constraints of these laws. Johnny is aware of a bitter irony in his father's fulminations against the white Administrator; he knows how difficult it is for his father to be anti-white, or even to conceive of being anti-white. The older man had spent his formative years in an atmosphere that allowed him a measure of political freedom and independence. He had the right to vote, he was active in union affairs, and he supported General Smuts's United Party. He tells his son: "I was brought up in a world where we always hoped for the best . . . I was a Smuts man, don't forget." Johnny knows his father still retains the basic attitudes of his younger days when there was some point in striving after social and political advancement: "He hopes too much," says Johnny. "He knows what the world is like, yet he goes on hoping. And when the blow comes it knocks him down." In reply to his mother's query "Don't you hope?", Johnny gives the militant response: "I hope for nothing . . . nothing, nothing, nothing. I hope for nothing that I won't get my own way." (T. 85, D. 17)

If the split between generations manifested in "Debbie Go Home" truly reflects the feelings of most of the Cape Colored People, then it suggests the approach of a new stage in South Africa's social evolution. The Cape Colored People, as a people of mixed blood, belong to the camp of neither the white nor the

black purists. As a minority group who can never hope to dominate the state, their inclination has been to associate themselves
with the group that does. They have, in fact, always had much
more in common with white South Africans than with indigenous
Africans, for although they are descended in part from African as
well as from European and Malayan forebears, they have no African cultural background. Some years ago a story appeared with a
South African setting, intended partly as a prophetic warning to
South African white supremacists, in which a Colored person is
represented as choosing to leave his group in an attempt to "pass
for black" rather than "for white" as his relatives had traditionally
done. The writer was suggesting that when Cape Colored People
began to make such a choice deliberately, then real power in
South Africa would have passed over from the whites to the non-
whites.

But Paton's "Debbie Go Home" looks more profoundly at the
conflict between generations of Colored people than the story
here referred to, which envisages the somewhat facile solution of
the gradual swing of power. The social and political system to
which Jim de Villiers' hopes of dignity and human significance
were wedded had, indeed, crumbled. He was a Smuts man; and
Smuts had always proclaimed that the Cape Colored People were,
in his own quaint phrase, "an appendage to the white race." But
Paton does not set young Johnny's program for the future against
his father's lost cause; nor does he represent Johnny's militancy as
more proper to the preservation of human dignity than his father's
acceptance of the supporting role in which Smuts condescend-
ingly cast the Cape Colored People.

The militant Unity Movement which Johnny supports is presumably the Non-European Unity Movement, a partly Trotskyite
group that drew some support from Colored intellectuals in the
Cape Province. This group opposed the programs of the African
Nationalist Congress in the 1950's as strongly as it opposed the
policies of the Afrikaner Nationalist Party. Its emergence at that
time can be interpreted as one of a number of symptoms that the
trend of South African history is toward a struggle between white
and non-white; Paton has remarked on this point: ". . . nor do I
know otherwise how to interpret the emergence of the tragic and
nihilistic movement known as the Non-European Unity Movement." [2]

Paton's story does not offer Johnny's nihilism, his cynicism, and his hopes for "nothing, nothing, nothing . . ." as preferable to his father's spiritlessness. Therefore, the lives of both father and son are equally tragic. "Debbie Go Home" offers no solution, unless it be the determination of Mrs. de Villiers to make the best of things —even to the extent of sending her daydreaming daughter to the Debutantes Ball: "There's many a hard thing coming to her as well. I'd like her to have one night, in a nice dress, and the coloured lights, dancing before the Administrator in the City Hall. We get kicks aplenty. I wanted her to have a boost." (T. 83, D. 16) Mrs. de Villiers, even though she suffers much, is not a tragic figure in the sense that her husband and son are. Their state is determined by a powerful outside force against which they react in opposite, but equally futile, ways. She relies on an inner force— a love that expresses itself in giving, without any thought of self. When she says: "Go your own way . . . But let me teach you one thing about giving. Don't keep half of it back," Johnny knows this is not the mere formula of words that his own proclaimed determination is: "I hope for nothing that I won't get my own way." Even he cannot resist the power of her inner force.

"Debbie Go Home" is a fine example of the storyteller's art, and it does not subordinate this art to some other purpose—whether such purpose be called social commentary or propaganda. The characters are unique human beings who are individual selves before they are South Africans or Cape Colored People or adherents of this or that political movement. Technically, "Debbie Go Home" is so close to the art of drama that it could be staged effectively without alteration.

"Debbie Go Home" mirrors one aspect of the life of an urban Colored family within the legal framework of the political theory called *apartheid*, or separate development. Its companion story on the Cape Colored People, "Life for a Life," is set in a rural area where relations between the races are traditionally based on the more primitive philosophy of separation called *Baasskap*. *Baasskap*, or Bossdom, is a social and political attitude that recognizes only one permissible relationship between white and non-white, and that is the master-servant relationship. The essential requirement of this relationship is that the servant should "know his place," and never aspire to equality on any ground.

In "Life for a Life," the central character, Enoch Maarman, a

Colored man of Hottentot descent, is head shepherd on the estate of Kroon. He is described as "a man who had never hurt another in his long gentle life, a man who like the great Christ was a lover of sheep and of little children." But by sending his son to the university, Enoch transgressed the fundamental law that required Colored shepherds to "teach their children to know forever their station." The master of Kroon, Big Baas Flip, therefore ordered that the shepherd's son should never again be permitted to set foot on his land, not even to visit his parents. When Big Baas Flip was found murdered, apparently by thieves who took away a heavy safe, the local police focused their investigation on the head shepherd who had brought suspicion on himself by failing to "know his place."

"Life for a Life" has two complementary sub-themes. One is embodied in a sadistic detective, Robbertse, who derives great pleasure from inflicting pain: "he hated to see any colored man holding up his head, he hated to see any colored man anywhere but on his knees or his stomach." Robbertse is more than a sadist; he has a touch of madness, real or feigned—an unreasoning hate that might be described as racial paranoia. Robbertse is not a type of the Afrikaner police officer, for when fellow officers are present they restrain him when he goes too far. He is a type of the extreme racist anywhere, who exhibits the apparently motiveless malignity with which deeply-rooted race hatred is sometimes expressed. To such a mind, persons of another race are inherently evil—as Jews were to Hitler, or as Othello may have been to Iago. And such a mind will, like Iago, take suspicion for surety. At nightfall, "which was no time to be looking for a safe," Robbertse came to carry out an earlier warning that Enoch would have to show him the place "where your friends hid the safe." Enoch does not return home from this expedition, and it is given out that he slipped in the river bed and crushed his head on a stone.

The second sub-theme is inherent in the efforts of Enoch's wife, Sara, to discover the exact cause of her husband's death and to recover his body, which has already been hurriedly buried. In the prevailing circumstances, Sara, like a character in a Kafka novel, is confronted by a vague power, malignant and irrational, that makes every rational step absurd. There are official answers to everything, but none of them fit.

Like Kafka's stories, "Life for a Life" is parable literature. It is a parable of *Baasskap* which, with men like Robbertse as its instrument, may condone brutality that "teaches a lesson." Brutality condoned involves others through complicity; so Enoch's death certificate states simply, *"death due to sub-cranial bleeding."* Police officers who would not themselves have harmed Enoch, accept without investigation the story that he slipped and fell, and they arrange hurried burial for the body on "an order from a high person." Paton's own summing up of one of Kafka's novels seems applicable here: "Kafka's story *The Trial* gives a frightening picture of the insignificance of man when he is confronted with the power of a cruel State. A man believing himself to be innocent is visited by the security police, taken to the court, tried by a judge who thunders at him, all this in such an atmosphere of fantasy and inexplicability that one realizes that one needs much more than innocence to save one from malignant authority." [3]

There is a suggestion of another dimension of parable in "Life for a Life." This arises from the explicit comparison of the head shepherd, Enoch Maarman, to the Good Shepherd, Christ: "a man who like the great Christ was a lover of sheep and of little children . . ." This comparison, made in the mind of Enoch's wife Sara, could be merely a conventional analogy. But there is also a suggestion that Enoch is an innocent victim demanded by the preservers of *Baasskap,* as the Chief Priests demanded Christ as a victim: "it is expedient that one man should die for the people." Or to express it as Paton did in his remarks on Kafka: "one needs more than innocence to save one from malignant authority." The Maarmans knew that with Big Baas Flip murdered: "Someone must pay for so terrible a crime, and if not the one who did it, then who better than the one who could not grieve." (T. 10, D. 46)

Even with this additional element of parable, it seems unlikely that Paton intends Enoch Maarman to represent Christ directly. He records that he once attempted, and rejected, a novel "about Christ's return to South Africa in the form of a young Afrikaner"; he is, therefore, aware of the difficulties of this form of fiction. If one examines "Life for a Life" in the light of the careful analysis of the literary problems of presenting Christ in novels or plays, on which Paton and Liston Pope collaborated in "The Novelist and Christ," it seems clear that the parallels between Enoch and Christ are limited to the indirection of parable, and that they do not constitute an attempt to present a symbolic figure representing Christ.[4]

Another of the stories in *Tales from a Troubled Land* provides a good contrast to "Life for a Life." This story, "A Drink in the Passage," represents an encounter between a young white Afrikaner and a young African, but its mood is far less somber than that of "Life for a Life." Indeed, it is Paton's lightest variation on one of his favorite themes: that of people of different races trying awkwardly, yet honestly, to reach out across barriers and touch each other as persons. Paton introduces us to an African journalist and sculptor, who relates his own story of how a young Afrikaner invited him to his home for a drink. There is awkward, fumbling good-will on both sides, but the young white man is completely unaware that in his attempt at comradeship he is, by honoring traditional custom, deeply embarrassing the African.

Lewis Nkosi, an African journalist formerly on the staff of the Johannesburg magazine *Drum*, says in his *Home and Exile* that Paton's story is a report of what actually happened in real life to one of the journalists associated with *Drum*.[5] The story is well done, and it provides another instance of Paton's liking for recasting actual events in fictional form for the sake of the light they shed on the human dilemma in South Africa.

The last of the non-reformatory stories in this collection of short fiction could also be described as Kafkaesque, but it might be linked even more appropriately with the work of Dostoevski or with Dante's *Inferno*. This very short story, "The Wasteland," is a masterpiece of artistic economy. In it, as in *Cry, the Beloved Country*, we encounter a society in which a code of conduct has been destroyed and not replaced by a better one. In this case, the sub-society of the urban juvenile gang provides the ultimate instance of cold-blooded dehumanization, for loyalty to the gang is demanded even above natural filial loyalty. The central character, like several other Paton characters, is a good man, hardworking and law-abiding, who falls victim to criminal attack. Returning home with his wages, he is waylaid in the dark by a gang that, as it turns out, includes his son. The situation has, indeed, the seeds of melodrama; but the story is told in such a cold shorthand of indirection and understatement that the reader is left to envision the ultimate horror of the encounter for himself. Again, as in *Too Late the Phalarope*, fear, foreboding, and terror are expertly evoked, and the cold-blooded inhumanity of the gang members is well shown. Just when they have come to believe that their victim and his money have eluded them, one of them stumbles over a dead body and calls out, in fine irony, "We are saved . . . here is the man." But the corpse is one of their own members, killed when their intended victim struck out blindly in his terror. And the hunted man hears again the name of his son as the gang members callously toss the body under the abandoned truck where their quarry is hiding.

This story envisions the ultimate inhumanity that is reached in a disintegrating society where law and custom have broken down, and which can only be restored through the reform of society itself. It should be compared with "Death of a Tsotse" in the Diepkloof stories.

III *The Diepkloof Stories*

Six of the ten stories in Paton's collected fiction are set in a reformatory. These are all told from the point of view of the principal of the reformatory, and at least some of them relate actual incidents that occurred during Paton's principalship at Diepkloof. Although they incorporate particulars of Diepkloof, their purpose is not autubiographical; and Paton has described the play *Sponono*, developed from three of these stories with the collaboration of Krisna Shah, as a story of reformatory life, not of his personal life.

These reformatory stories are chiefly character studies with an element of parable. Two of them, "The Worst Thing of His Life" and "The Elephant Shooter," are vignettes that present engaging portraits of white Afrikaner members of the reformatory staff. The remaining four are more elaborate psychological studies of young African inmates. The Principal, who appears as narrator in all of them, is not presented in a particularly good light, for they are all stories of his failures, or at best his limited successes.

Some reviewers, including Edward Weeks in *The Atlantic*, selected "Death of a Tsotsi" as the best of this group. For this reason, and also because its subject matter is similar to "The Waste Land" in the non-reformatory group, it may be useful to discuss it first. A *tsotsi* is a member of a juvenile African gang. The name *tsotsi* is an African corruption of the American term "zoot suit." The zoot suit was a forerunner of the leather jackets, or any similar fashion in clothing associated with youthful gangs in cities anywhere. Spike, the chief character in "Death of a Tsotsi," has a liking for flashy clothing; he even succeeds in livening up his reformatory uniform by wearing a red scarf on all occasions.

But as Paton's friend, Bishop Trevor Huddleston, has pointed out in *Naught For Your Comfort,* it is not the cut of the clothing that properly characterized the gangs of *tsotsis* in Johannesburg's African townships in the 1950's:

Today in Alexandra and Sophiatown . . . it is not the clothes, it is the number, the gang, the weapons which are so terrifyingly evident. The *tsotsi* is youth rotting away and rotting with fear the society around him. He is problem number one in urban Africa.[6]

The terrifyingly cold-blooded gang that Paton created in "The Waste Land" represents this rotting away to the point of ultimate inhumanity.

Spike, in "Death of a *Tsotsi,*" is a willing student at the reformatory. He attempts to break with his old gang and carries out his resolution to reform himself even in the face of threats from the gang members, who finally kill him rather than let him go free. Paton's parable in this story is the thesis he had put forward so frequently in his writings on penal reform: that the real cure for crime is reform of society itself. Pending such general reform, even successful restoration of particular individuals like Spike is almost impossible. The narrator says of Spike's death:

And this death would go on too, for nothing less than the reform of a society would bring it to an end. It was the menace of the socially frustrated, strangers to mercy, striking like adders for the dark reasons of ancient minds, at any who crossed their path. (T. 106, D. 69)

Another of the principal themes of Paton's writings on penal reform, the theme of the necessity for social significance, underlies the story "Ha'penny." This story characterizes a small, homeless waif, who seems to the Principal to have invented an imaginary family for himself but who, in fact, has "adopted" a real family that does not want him. The Principal decides to break Ha' penny's fantasy rather than have him face rejection again on his release from the reformatory. When the well-intentioned Principal reveals his knowledge of the facts to Ha'penny, "His whole brave assurance died within him, and he stood there exposed, not as a liar, but as a homeless child. . . . I had shattered the very foundations of his pride, and his sense of human significance." (T. 55, D. 31) The child falls ill and dies; and by his death, in a sense, passes judgment on the Principal, who had sensed "only the existence and not the measure of his desire" for human significance.

Stories of this kind present a certain difficulty for readers unfamiliar with the writer's intention. If the theme which the story is intended to dramatize is muted—and Paton tends to understate his themes—the reader may, understandably, take the story as presented for the sake of its inherent action. "Ha'penny" illustrates this difficulty, for it supplies a very small vessel for so large a theme as the importance of every man's desire for human significance. Once the reader has grasped Paton's parable, the story earns his respect; but if the point remains hidden from him, the story may seem merely melodramatic or sentimental.

The remaining Diepkloof stories, "Sponono" and "The Divided House," present characters strongly attracted to both good and evil who experience a struggle between the two sides of their natures. "Sponono," the longest of the Diepkloof stories, provides the core of the action for a three-act play of the same title written by Paton in collaboration with Krishna Shah. One interesting comparison between the short story and the dramatized version is that in the theater the theme becomes strikingly, almost shockingly, clear, whereas in the short story it forms little more than an undercurrent that does not disturb the surface.

The fictional character Sponono is based on an actual incorrigible who could not pass the final Diepkloof test of resisting temptation; yet who, by his charm and vanity, as well as his offenses and repentances, staked out a special claim to the Principal's attention. The name Sponono, which in Zulu means a beautiful, shapely woman, is presumably a nickname accorded him by his gangmates. Paton has described Sponono, "the boy with the silver tongue," as one who could "care for the weak, rob the unsuspecting, forgive his enemies, rape a girl, all in the compass of a single month. Many years after he wrote to me from prison, 'I wish now that I had listened to you.' " [7]

In one incident in this story, Sponono threatens and robs a couple picnicking in a lonely area of Diepkloof farm. This is apparently the same incident that Paton referred to many years before in a lecture on "The Prevention of Crime," where in making the point that people frequently invite crime through lack of foresight, he cited various instances, including this one: "A man wanders over to the Diepkloof farm and goes to sleep in the grass with fifty pounds in notes projecting invitingly from his hip pocket." [8]

The closeness of the fictional world of the Diepkloof stories to Paton's personal experiences makes it difficult to separate their artistic intention from their social purpose. Furthermore, publishers of his works have been only too ready to draw attention to Paton's humanitarian record in the social and political spheres, and thus, in a sense, present the stories primarily for the topicality of their social commentary.

On this problem of combining social conscience and artistic intention, Paton has very definite views. He says that the rules of writing and story-telling are inexorable, and that if they are broken the story fails:

> The inexorable rule is that you must put your story first, not your politics or your religion or your anger about the Group Areas Act. This does not mean that your politics or your religion must be left out of the story. On the contrary they inform the story and give it warmth and color and fire. But they must never usurp the place of the prime motive, which is to tell a story. [9]

A number of reviewers of *Tales from a Troubled Land* felt that Paton had not always succeeded in subduing his social purpose to his artistic intention in the stories in this collection; they therefore tended to give the author more credit for past performance than praise for the volume under review. The stories in the collection are uneven. Two or three of the Diepkloof stories, even though they illustrate some universal theme like the human need for recognition of worth, are more in the nature of incidents than plotted fiction with organic development. But several of the others come up to the standard Paton set in his two novels; and two or three achieve an intensity not common in the novels, and provoke speculation on what he might have accomplished additionally in fiction had his situation been otherwise.

IV *Paton's Achievement in Fiction*

Paton's collection of short stories seems likely to be the last of his books of fiction; for his career as a creative writer, that began with such promise in 1948, ended for all practical purposes when he was elected Chairman of the Liberal Party in 1956. In attempting to estimate his creative artistry on the basis of the novels and short stories he wrote during that short period, one thinks first of his regionalism. His art is related to South Africa as Robert Frost's is to New England. Both of these writers work within the framework of an external landscape where they know all flowers and shrubs, birds and animals, by their familiar names. As observers of the human inhabitants of these landscapes, both writers recognize the profound aspirations of human personality; and both communicate their insights in language that is fresh and simple, yet vibrant with meaning. While one may appropriately speak of the art of Paton or Frost as *regional,* it would be wholly inappropriate to speak of it as *provincial*—a term that suggests narrow interests or limited intellectual horizons.

The pull of *provincialism* is felt strongly by writers in South Africa, where each segment of the population is officially expected to confine its potential in any sphere to the requirements of its own group. For writers whose medium is Afrikaans or any of the African vernaculars, the problem of provincialism is additionally acute, since their potential audience may be fewer in numbers than the population of a medium-sized British or American city. To the world at large, therefore, South African literature is represented by the work of those poets and novelists of whatever racial background who write in English; and in the course of the past twenty years, South African writing in English has achieved recognition as a significant body of literature.

The forerunner was Olive Schreiner, whose *Story of an African Farm* (1883) had a world-wide reception similar to that later accorded to *Cry, the Beloved Country.* Interest in South African literature was revived in the 1920's and 1930's by Sarah Gertrude Millin's novels, particularly *God's Stepchildren,* and by the poet Roy Campbell and the novelist William Plomer, both of whom exiled themselves from South Africa. Two writers of Afrikaner lineage who did their best work while living outside South Africa also contributed to the growing reputation of South African writing in English. These are Stuart Cloete, whose novel *Turning Wheels* (1937) was banned in South Africa, and Laurens van der Post, whose early novel of African life, *In a Province,* and other later works, achieve a notable excellence of style even though

English is not his mother tongue. A few writers whose medium is Afrikaans have earned international recognition through their innate ability and their knowledge of literatures other than their own. The best known among these are the poet and dramatist Uys Krige, and the young poet Jan Rabie.

Since the end of World War II, South African writing in English has achieved a kind of Renaissance. Unquestionably, attitudes towards the racial policies that have focussed world attention on South Africa during this period have contributed to the interest in books from South Africa, and some works have been approved of, or condemned, more on non-literary than on literary grounds. Nevertheless, South African fiction writers in particular have responded with remarkable skill to the challenge of interpreting their country and to the literary expectations aroused by Paton's *Cry, the Beloved Country*.

It is not possible to treat the work of the post-war generation of South African writers justly, in summary form. Some, like the playwright Athol Fugard, whose *Blood Knot* was a New York success in 1964, and the novelist Nadine Gordimer, whose fiction has earned respect for acute observation and fluent craftsmanship, have assured reputations. Others have produced fine individual works like Harry Bloom's *Episode* or Daphne Rooke's *A Grove of Fever Trees*. In addition to these writers whose normal medium is English, some distinguished work has been produced by African and Colored writers. Peter Abrahams, who no longer lives in South Africa, is the most competent novelist in this group; but the young Cape Town writers, Richard Rive, Alex La Guma, and James Matthews have shown fine command of the short story as a form. Among the novelists who write in English yet portray African life through African eyes, three have begun to acquire reputations abroad: A. S. Mopeli-Paulus, Ezekiel Mphahlele, and Bloke Modisane. Modisane, whose work first appeared in the United States in *Atlantic*, commands a notably interesting and highly individual style, but it is too early, at present, to speculate on his probable achievement.

Several of this later generation of writers have been more productive than Paton, and several have produced work of unique artistic authenticity, but few have shown an equally profound insight into human behavior. It would be possible, for example, to transfer the substance of Paton's novels to settings in any continent or climate, and to re-people them with characters undifferentiated by color or race. His characters are universally recognizable because they are imbued with such universal qualities as courage, love, compassion, fear, or malice. The implications of his fictional themes are not limited, therefore, by their immediate South African circumstances. They scrutinize the universal human predicament.

CHAPTER 6

A Non-Racial Theater

I Nationalism and the Theater

FICTION and drama, as creative media, have some common elements, but they differ significantly in their manner of communicating with an audience. Fiction communicates to a reader alone, and, indeed, isolates him from his fellows while he is absorbed in it. Drama is a public act in which the spectator participates as one member of an audience composed of other people.

A man who objects to mingling with others in a theater audience may either choose to stay at home or to build a theater for himself and a few select friends. If he takes the latter course, he may then choose scripts and actors to meet his own taste, and so exclude any manifestations of reality that he considers unpleasant or uncongenial. In 1964 the Republic of South Africa enacted a law prohibiting theater audiences of mixed races. Such a law must inevitably affect the composition of drama itself. Dramatic works set in a multi-racial society must either mirror society as a whole, including the interaction among races, or they must exclude some aspects of society. To the extent that they do so as set policy, they limit their capacity to reflect the real world around them. It is, of course, possible, and artistically valid, to set a play or a novel in a limited segment of society; but it would be unrealistic to expect that no plays or novels should be set anywhere else.

Furthermore, plays with characters drawn from various races, as, for example, a dramatized version of *Cry, the Beloved Country*, raise the question of racially mixed casts. A gifted actor, as Sir Laurence Olivier has shown in his version of *Othello*, can portray a character of a different race with notable realism. But such competence is rare; and when the play has a localized modern setting familiar to an audience, as in the theoretical case of *Cry, the Beloved Country* presented in South Africa, authentic realism would be difficult to achieve with actors of one race taking all the parts. Presented before an African audience, such a production could hardly avoid a touch of unintentional comedy. It is on the basis of such artistic realities, as well as his determination to be "militantly non-racial" that Paton has declared: "I, myself, do not wish any play of mine to be presented before segregated audiences . . . Better no theatre at all than a colour-bar theatre." [1]

Paton has contributed to an attempt to bring into being in South Africa a non-racial drama countenancing racially mixed casts and integrated audiences. This adds a measure of historical significance to whatever intrinsic merit his plays may possess. He has not attempted dramatic forms on any substantial scale, despite the marked dramatic talent that characterizes his poetry and fiction. Besides the dramatizations of his novels done by other hands—*Cry, the Beloved Country* as a verse drama by Felicia Komai and *Too Late the Phalarope* by Robert Yale Libott—he has written three dramatic works that presuppose the possibility of a non-racial theater. At least part of his intention in writing these works was to give African actors scope for their talents.

The first of these plays, *Last Journey* (1959), deals with events following the death of Dr. Livingstone in May, 1873, when two of his African assistants, Susi and Chuma, accompanied by seventy-nine bearers, carried Livingstone's body from Ilala in the interior to Bagamayo on the coast, so that it could be taken by ship to Zanzibar, and thence to England for burial in Westminster Abbey. This journey across Africa took nine months to accomplish, and is believed to have cost ten lives.

Paton's purpose in *Last Journey* was not to present a historical drama focused on the epic journey for its own sake, but to present yet another variation on his familiar theme of restoration. To this end he recast the historical account into a fictional form designed to dramatize an act of reparation. Since *Last Journey* is unpublished and Paton has now no intention of publishing it, his purpose may be best illustrated by an excerpt from his "Author's Note" on the program for its first production at Lusaka:

It is true that although Acting Consul Prideaux received the body with appropriate ceremony, and although he thanked the bearers for their very great achievement, he left them all standing at Bagamayo; . . . his mind could not encompass the linking of this ragged band of heroes with the pomp and ceremony of Westminster. . . .

When it was learned that Susi and Chuma had been left behind in Africa, there was public demand that they be brought to England.

This was made possible by Mr. James Young of Scotland, one of Livingstone's most devoted admirers and friends. It was very important that this act of reparation should be recognized in the play, which otherwise would have ended on a sour note, displeasing, both to the audience and the playwright. However, it would have been dramatically difficult to have brought in at this stage a distant and unknown benefactor. Therefore, I chose Murphy to make the act of reparation, and he makes it symbolically by returning the sextant taken at Unyanyembe, and by staying at Bagamayo with the company instead of accompanying the body to Zanzibar. One kind of truth was thus sacrificed for the sake of another. . . . [2]

Last Journey was produced for the first time in Lusaka, Northern Rhodesia (now Zambia), in 1959. It was presented by the Waddington Players, an amateur group, with an interracial cast of twenty Africans and six Europeans, excluding walk-on parts. One commentator on this production drew attention to the problem of finding an English idiom that gives the flavor of a spoken African language. It will be remembered that this constituted one of Paton's triumphs in *Cry, the Beloved Country.* But H. Fosbrooke, writing in *The Northern Rhodesia Journal,* felt that the language of *Last Journey* had an alien ring to East African ears: "It jars on the ears of an East African to hear Southern Bantu idiom presented in English by Northern Rhodesian Africans purporting to be coastal Swahili." [3] Even though Paton has decided against publishing *Last Journey,* it merits attention as an instance of what he means by non-racial drama, and also for the significance of its theme: the recognition of human dignity and courage, and the need for reparation when such recognition has been denied.

Paton's second non-racial dramatic work was his libretto for the musical *Mkhumbane (Village in the Gully),* with music by Todd Matshikiza, which was specially written for the South African Institute of Race Relations, partly with the object of giving African actors and actresses a chance to display their gifts. *Mkhumbane* was first presented in Durban City Hall during the last week of March, 1960; a week that, by coincidence, was to be the week of greatest tension in recent South African history.

On Monday, March 21, 1960, police fired on crowds of demonstrators at Sharpeville in the Transvaal and Langa in the Cape Province. At Sharpeville, an African township adjacent to Vereeniging where the Boer War armistice had been signed, 69 Africans were killed by this police action, and 180 wounded. This tragedy initiated a period of intense fear and strife in South Africa. Ex-Chief Albert Luthuli, leader of the African National Congress, ceremoniously burned his Pass Book and called on all Africans to observe a day of mourning on March 28 by staying away from work. On that same day Parliament introduced an Unlawful Organizations Bill empowering the Government to ban the two African political organizations, the African National Congress and the Pan-African Congress. On March 30, the Government proclaimed a national State of Emergency; and, in the early morning of that day, the police detained 234 men and women of all races, including ex-Chief Luthuli and also Peter Brown, the National Chairman of Paton's Liberal Party.

Against this background, with thousands of Africans marching through the streets of Durban and Capetown, and with the white population of South Africa in a state of fear and anxiety, *Mkhumbane* was presented to mixed audiences in Durban. Paton recalls that "during this momentous week, we played to full houses, people of all kinds and races, in Durban City Hall. It was indeed a moving experience to go into that hall and see there the absence of all fear and hate." [4] This first production of *Mkhumbane* was successsful; but efforts to revive it in South Africa have not been successful because Todd Matshikiza's score, on which the musical depends more than it does on Paton's libretto, has been unavailable.

Besides the historic occasion of its first production, and its appeal to racially mixed audiences in South Africa, *Mkhumbane* has significance as an instance of the extraordinary vitality of the theater among Africans in South African cities during the 1950's and early 1960's. To say that *Mkhumbane* was written to give African actors and actresses a chance to display their gifts, means precisely that these actors were, in fact, gifted and that what they lacked was not talent, but suitable plays to perform.

By 1960 the music and drama school run by the Union of African Artists had produced an embarrassing amount of talent for the paucity of indigenous plays and musical pieces available. The quality of the products of this school may be measured by the success of the African jazz opera *King Kong* in London, where, with an all-South African cast, it had a successful six-month run. Or it may be measured by the quality of talent of individual graduates, like singer Miriam Makeba.

II Sponono

The fact that the theater workshop of the Union of African Artists had produced a core of trained African professional musicians and actors was brought to the notice of New York audiences by Paton's third play, *Sponono*. This play, adapted from his short stories with the collaboration of Krishna Shah, became the first South African show with original actors and producer to be transferred directly to Broadway after quite successful runs in Durban and Johannesburg.[5]

The first two acts of *Sponono* combine the action of the Diepkloof stories, "Sponono," "Ha'penny," and "Death of a Tsotsi." They introduce, in addition, a chorus of African singers and drummers and a clandestine court conducted by Sponono which tries reformatory offenders by having them submit to the primitive test of plunging their arms into a pot of boiling water.

Except for the presence of the chorus on stage throughout, these first acts follow the mode of conventional realistic drama. They take thirteen scenes to bring together the stories of several characters from the short stories; in a sense, therefore, both acts are an exposition preparing the way for the extraordinary, expressionistic trial scene that constitutes Act Three, "The Court." These opening acts also have certain qualities that distinguish them sufficiently from their narrative sources in the short stories to mark the play *Sponono* as a wholly separate work. The play departs from the sources in two respects: first, in the greater development of some characters; and second, by the addition of the Chorus, which helps to provide a unifying framework for the whole, and to expand the significance of the action on stage.

In the play, the character of the Principal assumes greater significance than in the Diepkloof stories—where the Principal as narrator suggests certain points of contact with the author as a person who once directed a reformatory. In the play, however, these points of contact disappear, and the Principal takes on another dimension in which his actions, in part, constitute a parable of that form of colonial rule in Africa frequently described as Christian Trusteeship; and, in part, the dilemma of any public man in a position of power who cannot choose his mode of behavior as freely as a good man in private life. Some other characters in the play are also more fully developed than their counterparts in the sources. For example, the opposing sides of Sponono's character are more sharply brought into contrast when he appears as "the first boy" and "the second boy," first welcoming, and then robbing a pair of unsuspecting visitors. The girl Elizabeth is developed from a mere shadow in "Death of a Tsotsi" to an appealing character in the play. And Walter, the unregenerate *tsotsi,* brings to the stage a measure of the cold inhumanity so skillfully manifested in the short story "The Waste Land."

Certain technical devices also enhance the dramatic quality of the play, but these depend largely on imaginative production for their effectiveness. The first is embodied in an imaginary Christmas scene or charade in which, for the benefit of the waif Ha'penny, the reformatory boys form a train and chug around in a circle with the accompaniment of chanting, stamping, and drumming, while the Chorus sings. The second is a scene completely without dialogue in which a gang of *tsotsis* knife Spike Moletsane to death. Howard Taubman, describing the Broadway production of *Sponono,* found this to be a melodramatic scene "that would not be out of place in a B film." [6] But Gene Cole, commenting on a Chicago production, found this scene to be the point where "the play itself (as distinguished from the surrounding pageantry) becomes gripping and promises to take some sort of shape." [7]

The most significant technical device introduced in *Sponono* is the Chorus of African drummers and singers. Without this Chorus *Sponono* would be a drama focused on the problem of choosing freedom or repression as a reformatory instrument. With the Chorus, the dilemma becomes that of Africa herself; for a Chorus of drummers and singers, irrespective of what they drum or sing, is African in association. In fact, no dramatic device could be more symbolic of Africa. Since the Chorus provides an authentic echo of the African scene, and traditional chants effectively establish an African atmosphere, the Chorus is not merely peripheral to the action but contributes an essential element to the final effect of the play. Throughout the action the Chorus hovers on the stage's edge, making the spectator conscious of Africa waiting to pass judgment on the Principal.

The third act of *Sponono* turns to expressionism. Here, in a dream sequence, the Principal is brought to trial before Sponono and charged with having deserted not only his duty, but also the principles of his own religion—particularly the admonition to forgive seventy times seven times.

In this trial scene, Sponono, although manacled, is enthroned as a judge surrounded by councillors, warriors, and drummers; all are in tribal costumes that suggest pre-colonial Africa as described by early explorers rather than the realities of Africa in the twentieth century. This scene, in which the boy passing judgment on the man personifies Africa judging her mentors, reaches an extraordinary pitch of dramatic intensity. Referring to this final scene in which "all the strands are brought together and woven into a dramatic texture that has profound impact and meaning," Howard Taubman said of the Broadway production: "Here *Sponono* becomes fused, takes fire, and justifies its transplantation from South Africa with its South African ensemble." [8]

Beyond the implications of its African setting, *Sponono* deals with a fundamental human dilemma at several levels. There is the dilemma of Spike, the member of a juvenile gang who honestly attempts to reform, but finds himself "caught between two ways and both ways dangerous." Since this phrase is repeated like a refrain by Spike and Elizabeth, it takes on some of the implications of the dilemma of fear and faith that underlies *Cry, the Beloved Country*. There is also the dilemma of Sponono attracted to the good, and to the Principal whom he feels represents the good, yet unable to comprehend the Principal's distinction between "forgiveness" and "bearing the consequences of an act." And there is the further dilemma of the Principal who espouses a religion that teaches forgiveness "unto seventy times seven," yet who, in an office of public trust, must trim his sails to what is possible and practical.

Sponono was successfully played by racially mixed casts before integrated audiences in Durban and Johannesburg during 1962 and 1963, prior to the enactment of the ban on mixed theater audiences in South Africa. It was transferred with its South African cast and producer to the Court Theater, New York, in April, 1964. Despite some favorable reviews stressing the play's significance—two of them by Howard Taubman in the *New York Times*—the play closed after a little more than two weeks, at a time when another South African play, Athol Fugard's *Blood Knot,* was enjoying a successful New York run.

One reviewer, Richard A. Duprey, blamed *Sponono's* tepid reception on the insensitivity of Broadway audiences:

In the play *Sponono* which has sadly and unaccountably closed here in New York, we see the dilemma of forgiveness and punishment bared in stirring, absolutely electrifying, dramatic form. This play . . . was so right and so eloquent it provides another in a sequence of sad closings, in a cultural *milieu* that seems to prefer sensation and trash to real insight and emotional excitement.[9]

A production of *Sponono* at the small Parkway Theater at Hull House, Chicago, provides an interesting contrast to the play's lack of success in Broadway's commercial theater. This Hull House production, directed by Michael Miller, played to full houses throughout its scheduled run of ten week-ends.[10] Richard Christiansen, reviewing the play for the *Chicago Daily News*, found *Sponono* to be "the damndest piece of theatre to be put on a Chicago stage this year." [11] He described it as "explosive, exciting, exuberant and smashingly singular in the kind of dramatic experience it offers." No doubt Michael Miller's imaginative production, and the professionalism of his drummers and dancers, contributed in good measure to this reviewer's enthusiastic response. But it is also worth noting that the Parkway Theater itself is a center for what Paton would call non-racial drama. In it, racially mixed casts play before integrated audiences who are, perhaps, more receptive to the work of Paton and Shah than Broadway audiences composed of conventional theater-goers.

III *Occasional Poems*

While he does not regard his occasional expressions in verse as constituting a claim to the title of poet, Paton has continued, from time to time, to publish poems. Unlike the undergraduate verse discussed in a previous chapter, these later poems draw almost exclusively on South African life and attitudes for their subject matter. These poems may be classified in three categories: first, some lyric portraits of aspects of African life; second, a few satirical verse commentaries aimed at conventional white South African assumptions and the theory of *apartheid;* third, a number of religious poems.

The four poems included in *A Book of South African Verse,* "Sanna," "The Discardment," "Samuel," and "To a Small Boy who Died at Diepkloof Reformatory," are good examples of the first category.[12] Each gives an apparently simple portrait of an African character, but beneath the surface simplicity there is a indirect commentary with considerable ironic bite.

The vein of apparent satire in these poems is developed in two other poems of this period: "Apartheid," and "My Great Discovery." The poem "Apartheid" first appeared in *Salute to My Greatgrandchildren,* a book in which Paton attempts to examine the implications of a liberal approach to South Africa's social problems through the device of letters addressed to his greatgrandchildren in the twenty-first century. "Apartheid" [13] presents a glowing but ironic picture of the ideal of Separate Development which aims to restore Bantu institutions and culture. "My great Discovery" is a lighter piece comprising about 130 lines of satirical doggerel on the fortunes of a scientist who discovered a simple method for changing the pigmentation of any nation. It includes brief satirical portraits of some members of Dr. Verwoerd's cabinet.[14]

For his meditative, or religious, poems, Paton has come to use a metrical form based on the cadences of the Psalms. Two of these, "I have seen my Lord in the forest . . ." and "My Lord has a great attraction for the humble and simple . . . ," were both published with the title of "A Psalm." A longer poem in the same metrical manner, *Meditation for a Young Boy Confirmed,* has been published in Britain as a separate booklet.[15] This poem is a meditation on the relevance of Christian faith and its liturgical forms to twentieth century life, and it is addressed to Paton's son Jonathan on the occasion of his confirmation. It was probably written in 1950 during one of Paton's absences from South Africa. Horton Davies quotes from it as an unpublished poem in "Alan Paton: Literary Artist and Anglican" (1952). This poem appeared in *The Christian Century* in October, 1954, and in *Theology* in August, 1958, before its separate publication as a booklet by the London Society for Promoting Christian Knowledge.

Two others among Paton's occasional poems of this period are likely to remain part of his permanent literary record, even though he does not intend to publish a book of poems. One of these, "Toll iron bell, toll extolling bell . . . ," a poem on the death

of Jan Hofmeyr, has been included in the biography *Hofmeyr*.[16]
The second, "I Have Approached a Moment of Sterility," is memorable for its expression of Paton's purpose as a writer, which he once described as a desire to write books that would stab South Africa in the conscience. This poem on the impulse to shape language into literary forms concludes with this address to words:

> Therefore words, stay where you are awhile
> Till I am able to call you out,
> Till I am able to call you out with authentic voice
> So that the great living host of you
> Tumble out and form immediately
> Into parties, commandos, and battalions
> Briefly saluting and wheeling away instantly
> To waken the sleeping consciences
> To call back to duty the absenting obligations
> To assault again, night and day, month and year,
> The fortress and bastions of our fears.[17]

The full text of this poem has been included in *The Long View*, a collection of Paton's writings published in the United States in 1967.

CHAPTER 7

A Biographic Symphony: Hofmeyr

I *No Ivory Tower*

FOR some years Paton's literary reputation has rested on two successful novels and a handful of short stories. But the judgment of the future may rank his recent biography of Jan Hofmeyr as a literary achievement equal to the novels and possibly surpassing them. Since some aspects of Hofmeyr's influence in Paton's work have already been discussed in earlier chapters, it may suffice to recall here that Jan Hofmeyr was a superb administrator under whose leadership white South Africans seemed inclined to move toward the goal of a common society.

With extended interruptions, Paton worked on his biography of Hofmeyr over a period of fifteen years between Hofmeyr's death in December, 1948, and the completion of the manuscript in March, 1963. The plan for this book was in incubation for an even longer period. Paton wrote his first biographical sketch of Hofmeyr, "Jan Hendrik Hofmeyr—An Appreciation," in 1936,[1] and he records that at some time during World War II he told Hofmeyr that he would one day write his life. Hofmeyr, he adds, did not show great enthusiasm, but said: "I think you could." [2]

Paton believed that if he could write any life it would be Hofmeyr's. He knew Hofmeyr's home and his mother, and also something of the relationship that bound mother and son so closely. He had long shared Hofmeyr's interest in the work of the Students' Christian Association and he was familiar with the side of Hofmeyr's complex personality displayed at the annual boys' camps. While he was not privy to political decisions involving Hofmeyr as a member of the cabinet and as Deputy Prime Minister, he was aware that the conflict between Hofmeyr and his parliamentary opponents had deeper roots than party politics. However well qualified Paton was to write a biography of Hofmeyr, the undertaking became, eventually, one of the most difficult and time-consuming tasks he ever set his hand to. Since the difficulties that prevented early completion of the biography also account for his failure to produce any other major creative work after *Too Late the Phalarope,* it may be advantageous to review his circumstances.

Reflecting on the reasons that may prevent a writer from regularly producing new works, Paton's fellow South African, William Plomer, remarks that the most important of these is life itself, which may "impose such duties, exert such stresses, or bring such fulfilments upon a writer that it absorbs those creative energies which might have been given to art." [3] Plomer's estimate fits Paton's case exactly. The success of *Cry, the Beloved Country,* and the interest it aroused, had encouraged Paton to devote his time to the creative task of interpreting South Africa through the medium of literature. He therefore retired from the state service as principal of Diepkloof Reformatory in 1948; and he gave some of his reasons for doing so in a broadcast talk:

I have left the Public Service, but not with any intention of living in idleness or ease. I want to interpret South Africa honestly and without fear. I cannot think of any more important or exciting task. All my life, of course, I have lived actively in a world of problems and people, and I do not know if I shall be able to live the kind of life an author seems to find necessary. This is one of the things I must find out for myself. [4]

Paton was given little chance to enjoy the kind of seclusion from the world of problems and people that his creative muse seemed to demand. Even before the year 1948 had ended, Jan Hofmeyr died. His last injunction, whispered to his brother, was: "Tell my friends to carry on." Hofmeyr's death, on December 3, 1948, left the road ahead full of uncertainties for those who had hoped he would be the mainstay of the liberal cause in South Africa. Paton felt his death keenly. As a private man he could not "carry on" Hofmeyr's work in public affairs, but he was better qualified than others in Hofmeyr's circle to write his biography, and he immediately began making preparations for doing so.

At first the work went well. In the early stages he lived with Hofmeyr's mother, Mrs. Deborah Hofmeyr, then aged eighty-eight, and "learned the true version of many legends." But his reluctance to rely on her viewpoint alone and his determination to ferret out others, whether friend or foe, who were familiar with facets of Hofmeyr's career, displeased her. She began to take a dislike to the idea of a biography that proposed to be anything more than a record of her son's public career. It became clear to Paton that the kind of biography he envisaged, particularly one that would "relate her own tremendous role in her son's life," could not be published while she was alive. So in 1952 he laid the work aside for the time being.

Mrs. Hofmeyr lived for seven years after they parted. When she died, aged 95 on July 27, 1959, Paton took up the work again; but by then he admits he was "no longer a pure writer, having felt it a duty to follow Hofmeyr's course and collaborate with Margaret Ballinger, Leo Marquard, Jordan Ngubane, Peter Brown and others, in the work of the Liberal Party, founded in 1953." It took almost four more years of work to complete the book. During this time there were further interruption, of which the most serious was the State of Emergency during 1960, when Peter Brown was imprisoned and Paton had to act as National Chairman of the Liberal Party. He refers to this time of trials in an essay, "The Hofmeyr Biography," [5] but he omits mention of the fact that the unfinished manuscript of the biography "spent part of its life hidden lest police should raid and take it away." [6]

Although these delays were irksome, Paton does not now regret them. He feels that the lapse of time permitted him to take a more mature view of a man for whom he had a deep affection. In this he is undoubtedly right, for if one compares the appreciation of Hofmeyr in Paton's *Salute to My Greatgrandchildren*, written in 1952, with the character study set forth twelve years later in the biography, one finds a far greater degree of objectivity and mastery of personal emotion; what might have been a source of weakness is transformed into a strength.

II *An Inner Drama*

In the final analysis Paton's personal relation with Hofmeyr helps to make this work a representative example of what the art of biography can accomplish in our age. Our art is characterized by its ability to portray the inner life, which cannot be deduced from the public record. The poet W. H. Auden has remarked on how modern literature has forsaken the public sphere as the realm of revealing personal deeds. And he adds that to write a good poem on Winston Churchill a poet would have to know Churchill intimately, "and his poem would be about the man, not the Prime Minister." [7]

Paton's *Hofmeyr* is, essentially, about the man whose lot was to become Deputy Prime Minister for a time and afterwards to be rejected. It meets the requirements for revelatory biography to a unique degree; for in it a novelist of marked talent explores the strengths and weaknesses of the inner spirit of a public man whom he knew intimately in the private sphere. Commentators have not yet come to grips with Paton's *Hofmeyr* as a modern biography. Instead, they have focused their attention on it largely as a record of Jan Hofmeyr's achievement in the political realm. Significantly in this regard, the title chosen for the American version of this work, *South African Tragedy: The Life and Times of Jan Hofmeyr,* emphasizes the book's relevance to South Africa's political situation and underplays the personal element.

Although Paton was Hofmeyr's friend for many years and a great admirer of his moral courage,the biography was not persevered with through years of difficulties simply out of friendship or admiration. There were those who thought that "of all the lives waiting to be written, Hofmeyr's was the least promising—dull, virtuous, conventional, with no wine, women, or song." Paton, with a novelist's discernment, realized that on the contrary Hofmeyr's life had "an inner drama as exciting as anything to be found in South Africa." [8] This inner drama might have proved reason enough to undertake the work, but Paton had a more compelling reason. He was convinced that the story of Hofmeyr's life could reveal the true spirit of South Africa in our times more clearly than the biography of any other public figure, including Field Marshal Smuts.

Hofmeyr's biography does not assume this importance as a direct outcome of his personal qualities, or of any lasting achievements of his liberal spirit. Paton takes pains to point out that Hofmeyr's liberalism was characterized by cautious advances and conservative retreats, and that many of the categories of his thought are already outmoded and bear little relevance to the realities of present-day Africa.

Even had Hofmeyr never lived, the story of South Africa in our times would have been a story of conflicting views on whether increased freedom or more narrow restrictions should shape society in that multiracial land. This conflict in the soul of white South

Africa between the Spirit of Liberty and the Spirit that Denies, always emerges in the civil sphere as a struggle between liberal and repressive attitudes towards the civil liberties of the non-white majority. Hofmeyr saw this conflict clearly, and stated it straightforwardly when he said in 1938 that: "in the mind of the average white South African there was a struggle between the desire to be just and the fear of being just. Yet fear produces hatred and hatred produces disaster. Therefore one must go forward in faith not fear." [9] In 1946, in a Commencement address at the University of the Witwatersrand, he appealed for the addition of a fifth freedom—freedom from prejudice—to the four freedoms of the Atlantic Charter. This address became know as Hofmeyr's *Herrenvolk* speech, because in a direct allusion to Nazi racism he declared, "The plain truth, whether we like it or not, is that the dominant mentality in South Africa is a Herrenvolk mentality." He went on to say that prejudice was South Africa's hallmark. He warned of its consequences for the country's economic progress and concluded:

But our chief loss is a moral loss. As long as we continue to apply a dual standard in South Africa to determine our attitudes towards . . . European and non-European on different ethical bases, to assign to Christian doctrine a significance which varies with the colour of a man's skin, we suffer as a nation from what Plato would have called the lie in the soul—and the curse of Iscariot may yet be our fate for our betrayal of the Christian doctrine which we profess.[10]

Hofmeyr's *Herrenvolk* speech also contained a warning against "the growing tendency to describe as Communist . . . any who asked for fair play for all races or who suggested that non-Europeans really should be treated as the equal of Europeans before the law." Yet only a few years after his death, this "tendency to describe" was translated into a tendency to proscribe under the Suppression of Communism Act broadly interpreted.

During the fifteen years of his South African parliamentary career, Hofmeyr became identified with the Spirit of Liberty. One aspect of his story significant for the world at large, therefore, lies not in the measure of how modest or how exemplary his liberalism was in practice, but in how the mere sight of it provoked the Spirit that Denies to fortify the citadel of racial intolerance. The political conflict that embroiled Hofmeyr had sensitive well-

springs running deeper than differences in social or political outlooks. Hofmeyr's belief that South Africa should aspire toward a
common society recognizing the human significance of all men
was based on his Christian convictions. But his parliamentary opponents—supporters of a political ideal which they called "Christian Nationalism"—differed radically from him in their conception
of Christianity. Paton characterizes the more extreme among them
as "outraged believers in that heretical Christianity which has
made a racial separation the highest of all goods, and racial difference a God-given gift which no ordinary man could set aside."

Because of this fundamental difference in outlook, their inevitable clash with Hofmeyr attained the uncompromising intensity of
a holy war, waged openly under the slogan provided by J. G.
Strijdom, a later Prime Minister: "Hofmeyr must be destroyed." It
is in this context that Hofmeyr's story, as Paton pointed out to
Studs Terkel in an interview, becomes the story of our times:

Hofmeyr's story is *the* story of our times in South Africa—even more
than the biography of Jan Smuts—because he not only tried to resist
the drift to authoritarianism and neofascism but he proclaimed his
Christian principles when it came to racial questions. Looking back
from today one sees that Hofmeyr is very likely outdated—things
move too fast—but that doesn't alter the fact that he was the obstacle
to the realization of present policies. Hofmeyr was a minister in Smuts's
government, and in any normal society he would have been his suc-
cessor, but he couldn't because he split his own party with his views
on racial affairs. The United Party feared that if Hofmeyr continued
he would drive all the right wingers into the Nationalist Party and,
although Hofmeyr died before that occurred, that is precisely what
has happened: the right wing of the United Party was taken over by
the Nationalists.[11]

III *The Evolution of a Statesman*

When Jan Hofmeyr was eighteen, he wrote the official biography of his famous uncle, Jan Hendrik Hofmeyr, who was a leading political figure in the nineteenth century Cape parliament, an
opponent of Cecil Rhodes, and the founder of the Afrikaner
Bond. Paton describes this biography as a painstaking account of
every event in which the elder Hofmeyr took part. But he notes
that "of the man it said nothing," that it showed no gift for psychological observation, and that it failed to reveal the relationship

between Cecil Rhodes and the elder Hofmeyr in any dramatic form. This commentary on Jan Hofmeyr's youthful attempt at biography is, indirectly, a commentary on his own biographical method. Paton's biography recounts the events, but it is not a conventional record of a public man's career. It never loses sight of the manner of man Hofmeyr was, and, in particular, how he became what he was.

Hofmeyr's progress emerges in several related dramas. There is the main drama of Hofmeyr the protagonist of the liberal spirit, who becomes, in a sense, a tragic victim. This main action is supported by other unfolding dramas. There is the drama of his relationship with his mother and the drama of his relationship with General Smuts, his distant kinsman and long his Prime Minister. There is the inner drama of his self-emancipation from custom and inbred prejudice, and the drama of his spiritual journey from the certainties of a narrow dogmatism to the accepted uncertainty of going forward in faith—"alone, out over seventy thousand fathoms," as Kierkegaard put it—with no guide but his Christian convictions. Finally there is the drama stemming from these very convictions which emerges as the dilemma of political life—the problem of acting justly in the treacherous area between principle and expediency.

Jan Hofmeyr was first of all an intellectual prodigy. When he was only five years old it was discovered that he had taught himself to read in both English and Dutch, and that he could repeat verbatim the sermons he heard in church. He began school at the age of eight and completed the whole elementary and secondary curriculum within four years. At twelve he went on to the university, and at fifteen he received his B. A. with first-class Honors. Such progress was spectacular but one-sided. He was intellectually superior to his classmates at the university, but in other aspects he was a mere child among adults, and his mother insisted that he dress as a child. He was therefore isolated from more mature fellow students, particularly in emotional or social attachments. Since his interest was solely in intellectual achievement, his other aptitudes are poorly developed, and all his life he lacked that quality "which responds to music or poetry or painting or drama." He also lacked interest in his personal appearances, and became notorious for the carelessness and untidiness of his dress.

Hofmeyr's father died when he was two years old. From that

time on, his life became inextricably entwined with his mother's love and domination. Mrs. Hofmeyr loved her son fiercely and exclusively, and cared for him tirelessly. She was a forthright, outspoken, and strong-willed woman. Paton invariably describes her will in such terms as *indomitable, implacable,* and *imperious:* "Her will was implacable . . . one either capitulated to it or got out of her reach." She was also a devoutly religious woman with a strict puritanical spirit that weighed infidelity to moralities great or small in equal scale. Yet she enjoyed malicious gossip and was noted for her cutting tongue. Her love for her son was genuine, but she failed to distinguish between love and possessiveness. Hofmeyr soon learned that the price of his mother's devotion was his devotion; any attempt to break free "would create such crisis of recriminations, claims, self-pityings, and other ugliness, that he could not have borne it."

Hofmeyr never broke from his mother, but he did try to wean himself from her possessiveness and he gradually established an autonomous area—the realm of public affairs—where he was sole master. Otherwise they remained "inseparably joined together like Siamese twins of the spirit." The spirit of Mrs. Hofmeyr broods over Paton's biography in something like the same degree that she herself held sway over her son's life as she cared for him, yet betrayed jealousy beyond reason of his infinitesimal sallies toward other women. But in death the son finally parted from the mother under the cloud of her displeasure. In the last days of his life he disobeyed her—foolishly as it turned out—to undertake some minor duties when she felt that his poor health would not permit such activity.

Paton emphasizes the drama of Hofmeyr's struggle to wean himself from his mother's possessive love, but he unfolds with even greater care the drama of Hofmeyr's struggle to emancipate his mind from white South African prejudices. His account of Hofmeyr's first year at Oxford University portrays a young man with a marked capacity for puritanical intolerance. Hofmeyr was not only shocked by student drinking, but he tended to describe any show of conviviality as drunkenness. He was shocked, too, at first, by the absence of the familiar color-bar, and he admitted to a close friend: "I was rather shocked when I got there that just next to me was an Indian named S——, even more so when another Indian asked me to breakfast with him and I had to go. It is rather

hard getting used to different ideas about colour just at first."
Later, however, Hofmeyr rid himself of anti-Indian prejudice and
developed a friendship with J. Matthai, an Indian fellow student
who was subsequently a Minister in Nehru's first cabinet. Commenting on Matthai's influence on Hofmeyr, Paton is moved to
remark: "Unfortunately there were no African students with
whom he had anything to do, because undoubtedly he would
have learned from these relationships also."

Other stages in Hofmeyr's self-emancipation are fairly easy for
the biographer to identify and elaborate on. There are the instances, for example, when he took a public stand on liberal principles either in parliament or in his writings; and at times his letters and private papers give hints on his inner progress. Hofmeyr
lacked personal contact with Africans, and this makes it difficult
for the biographer to trace changes in his personal feelings toward
them. There was only one place where Hofmeyr experienced anything approaching social contact with Africans, and that was Fort
Hare Native College. Paton feels that Fort Hare exercised a
strong influence on Hofmeyr, and says, "it was there that he made
some of his most daring leaps into the unknown." Paton's description of one event at Fort Hare may be of particular interest here,
in view of the parallels drawn earlier in this book between Paton's
account of his own deep experience at the funeral service for
Edith Rheinallt Jones and the related significances of the funeral
service for Arthur Jarvis in *Cry, the Beloved Country*. He describes this event in language that can only imply that Hofmeyr
shared a similar deep experience at the outset of his political career.

In 1930, Hofmeyr, then a member of parliament, went to Fort
Hare Native College to open a joint Bantu-European Student
Christian Conference. His theme was "unity in Diversity," and he
expressed the hope that the gain of one group in South African
Society should not be secured at the cost of another. Paton speaks
of this inter-racial conference as a visible manifestation of the
kind of racial unity and harmony that might be possible in South
Africa. In particular he refers to a joint Communion service,
"which may have been the first ecumenical and interracial service
of that size ever to be held in South Africa." When he elaborates
on how this service affected the participants, some of his statements parallel, word for word, his description of his own deep

experience at the funeral service for Mrs. Edith Rheinallt Jones described in Chapter 2, above.

Paton says that for some this inter-racial service "was the deepest experience of their lives," and he continues in the exact words of "A Deep Experience": ". . . *and who knows how many years must pass and how many lives be spent and how much suffering undergone before it all comes true. And when it all comes true, only those who are steeped in the past will have any understanding of the greatness of the present.*" [12]

Whether or not Hofmeyr shared this deep emotional experience, Paton has good reason for suggesting that this Student Christian Conference in 1930 marked a stage in Hofmeyr's evolution to a non-racial attitude. He later makes it clear that 1930 was the year in which Hofmeyr abandoned thoughts of an ideal separation of the races in South Africa and set his foot firmly on the road toward a common society.

If 1930 was a significant year for Hofmeyr's inner development, 1936 was an even more significant year for him in the arena of public life. In that year he risked an open break with his Cabinet colleagues by opposing important government legislation affecting the voting rights of Africans in the Cape Province. His opposition to this legislation might have been expected, but not, perhaps, the grounds on which he opposed it. He attacked this legislation as an abuse of white power, and thus challenged the whole concept of segregation. From then on the champions of white supremacy identified him as their chief antagonist. Thereafter they disseminated the myth that he was not a reformer, but a militant and crusading revolutionary determined to hand power over to the black population.

IV *Between Principles and Expediency*

One of the principal dramatic themes of Paton's biography is the dilemma of the private man who must trim his personal ideals to the exigencies of public office. The crucial instance of this revolves about the question of why Hofmeyr did not found a Liberal Party. The problem is a complex one with bearings on his relationship to General Smuts, his relationship with other liberals, and his personal capacity for leadership; but at least part of the answer rests on the inescapable conclusion that some gains could be made within the framework of the United Party which held office, while none at all might be made by a splinter Liberal Party out of office. Since Hofmeyr did not raise the liberal banner himself, the question of the depth and sincerity of his liberal commitment is unanswerable. But one can, perhaps, measure it in terms of a parallel instance of the difference between his private ideals and what he thought publicly expedient.

One reason why the humanitarian-minded were displeased with Hofmeyr's seeming parsimony in the area of African education while he was Minister for Finance was that they believed him to be very keenly interested in supporting education for Africans. The sums of public money he put aside for this did not seem to them in keeping with his reputation. Yet the cause of African education lay near Hofmeyr's heart, and if his public expenditures do not bear this out his private arrangements do.

Hofmeyr and his mother lived frugally all their lives. They even succeeded in saving a substantial sum from his Rhodes Scholarship money while at Oxford. Hofmeyr had no private means. He delayed his entry into politics until he thought he had saved enough from his salary to make him financially independent. Later, when he felt his savings would provide modestly for himself and his mother in their retirement, he established a private trust fund, which he called the Deo Gratias fund, to be used for the advancement of African education. Into this fund Hofmeyr paid four-fifths of his ministerial salary each year. And he made this sacrifice, as Paton puts it, "out of thanks to God for the mercies of his mother and his honours and his industrious life." After his death the money in this fund was handed over to the Jan Hofmeyr School of Social Work, started by the YMCA to open up social work as a profession for African men and women.

Over against this personal commitment there is the record of Hofmeyr's public achievement. Traditionally in South Africa, the education and welfare of the African population were financed by special taxes on Africans and not from the general revenue, which was thought of as "white tax money." Traditionally, too, per capita expenditures followed a discriminatory scale geared to the standard of living of each group. The public expenditure on each white child in school, for example, was approximately seven times greater than the expenditure on each African child.

The legislation affecting Africans that Hofmeyr introduced during his terms of office rejected one of these traditional principles but not the other. We have already seen in the discussion of the origin of Diepkloof Reformatory how the improvements introduced by his Children's Act of 1935 applied equally to children of all races. In subsequent years he introduced legislation financing education for African children out of the general revenue, and establishing the practice that money for African schools be distributed through the national Department of Education and not through the Department of Native Affairs. Again, when he introduced legislation in old age pensions and social welfare benefits, he saw to it that these benefits were extended to all races although he accepted the traditional discriminatory scale of payments.

In these respects Hofmeyr made gains towards establishing principles for a common society but not towards equal social justice. The actual sums of money from the common budget expended on African education were small, partly because South Africa was on a wartime economy and partly because the opposition even within his own party would not permit him larger sums. The small practical gains caused Africans to doubt the sincerity of his liberal commitment, and this doubt seemed justified in view of another impasse that was painful for Hofmeyr. In 1946, while General Smuts was attending the United Nations meetings at Lake Success, it fell to Hofmeyr as Acting Prime Minister to respond to the demands of the Natives' Representative Council for alleviating the effects of discriminatory laws. Hofmeyr had to refuse to accede to the Council's demands even in the face of its determination to boycott subsequent sessions. Paton sees this event as a turning point in South African history. "After that," he says, "the demand of non-white people was for equality, not alleviation . . . And Hofmeyr, in the eyes of many non-white people, ceased to be the spokesman of freedom and became the spokesman for white supremacy. He knew it, and found it painful."

Paton's interest in the dilemma of a man of strong principles in an office of public trust has parallels in his creative writing. This dilemma supplies the essential theme of *Sponono* and Paton has referred to the parallel in responding to a question about the play. Of the conflict between Sponono and the Principal he says, "Finally, the boy passes judgment on the man. What is involved is the difficulty of carrying out the Christian injuction to forgive until seventy times seven—especially when you are in a position of power and authority." Paton then goes on to draw the parallel with Hofmeyr:

Hofmeyr is a case in point: a man with great Christian principles he was also Deputy Prime Minister and had to go to our Natives' [Representative] Council here to tell them he could not remove discriminatory laws. I think we must accept the fact that the good private individual must behave somewhat differently when a public man. No use weeping over that. If you are going into politics and accept a position of power you must trim your sails . . .[13]

V *The Art of Biography*

Literary biography is a higher art than chronology or chronicle. A chronicle is a straight-line record of events in time from the beginning to the end, but a literary biography may attain the multifaceted unity of a rose-window or a musical symphony. Paton's *Hofmeyr* could be approached, for example, as a gallery of portraits composed with a novelist's skill. Besides the dominating pictures of Hofmeyr, his mother, and General Smuts, there are perceptive portraits of the major architects of Afrikaner nationalism: General Hertzog, Dr. Malan, Mr. Strijdom, and Dr. Verwoerd. In addition to his revealing pictures of its leaders, Paton succeeds perhaps better than any other writer in evoking the emotional atmosphere that supplied much of the impetus for the rise of Afrikaner nationalism in the decade between 1938 and 1948. His account of the celebrations of the centenary of the Great Trek in 1938, for example, shows how the genuine emotional forces released by this dramatic re-enaction of the heroic Afrikaner past were harnessed to the service of nationalism.

If one approaches this biography simply as a chronology of the times, certain events that Paton places emphatically in the foreground may seem to receive disproportionate attention. Such an instance is the chapter "The Stibbe Affair," which recounts one of Hofmeyr's adminstrative failures as Principal of the University. Hofmeyr dismissed a highly-regarded professor in circumstances strongly suggesting that he had acted harshly on insufficient evidence. The University senate championed the cause of the dismissed professor and a long drawn out conflict with Hofmeyr ensued. Considered as part of the story of South Africa in Hofmeyr's times, this incident hardly deserves the extraordinary research Paton put into getting the account right. But the chapter is, in fact, a key section of the biography of Hofmeyr the man who might have founded a Liberal Party in South Africa. As it happened, the members of the University faculty most affronted by Hofmeyr's action included those who then were, or who later became, outstanding proponents of the liberal cause in South Africa:

Thus were alienated the Rheinallt Joneses, the Hoernlés, and Margaret Hodgson [Mrs. Ballinger], five of the outstanding South African liberals of the time, all dedicated to the same cause as Hofmeyr, and the same principles, all alienated by the Stibbe affair from the man who was to become the spearhead of the revolt against the policies of white supremacy and apartheid. (H. 104, S.A.T. 75)

Paton composed his *Hofmeyr* of forty chapters strung on the hub of historical continuity, but designed also to bring into focus the complete interaction between a man's self-experience and the external pressures of life. Even the titles of his chapters are chosen to this end. There may be many possible titles for the opening chapter of a biography, but for the unique life lived by Jan Hofmeyr there is only one appropriate opening and that is Paton's "Mother and Son." Again, the title of the final chapter, "To His Captain's Pavilion," even though at first it may seem a trite repetition of the commonplace reference to the cricketer returning to the stands after completing his inning at bat, has peculiar appropriateness. It is, in the first place, the final line of a poem, "Toll iron bell extolling bell," that Paton composed on the death of Hofmeyr. Hofmeyr's love of cricket, even though he was not very good at it, is an inescapable fact, and the last act of his life took place on the cricket field where he collapsed in an attempt to carry out the trivial duty of ceremoniously opening the play. He liked to be one of the "Eleven," as a cricket team is called, and that is why Paton gives the title "One of the Eleven" to the chapter that recounts his rebellion against his party in 1936, when his was one of the eleven votes cast against the bill removing African voters from the common roll. Yet, even though Paton leaves no doubt about who Hofmeyr's Captain was, "To His Captain's Pavilion" may seem a lighthearted label for an account of the death of a great man. In seeming to accept Hofmeyr's death lightly, Paton is simply insisting on the acceptance of Hofmeyr's death as a reality to be faced, and turning away from useless speculation on the trend of events "if Hofmeyr had lived." He responds to the question often asked, "What if Hofmeyr had lived?" by saying, "If he had lived with the same body and the same *malaise* he would not have lived long. . . . Hofmeyr was not struck down in the prime of life; he was struck down—and I write this gravely—at the end of it." [14] Paton does not, of course, take Hofmeyr's death lightly. His account of it includes the only passages in the biography where he permits himself to reveal his emotion in poetic eloquence:

So a great light went out in the land, making men more conscious of its darkness. It was a light of a man not radiant by nature but by character . . . On the morning of December 4 tens of thousands of hearts were filled with unspeakable grief, not only because they had loved him, but because he was the man who had been to them "as a hiding place from the wind . . . as the shadow of a great rock in a weary land." (H. 525; S.A.T. 410)

VI South African Tragedy

Paton's *Hofmeyr* was published in the United States in October, 1965, in a slightly abridged version with the title *South African Tragedy: The Life and Times of Jan Hofmeyr*. This abridgment by Dudley C. Lunt reduces the original book of some 550 pages by about one-fifth. It adds an informative "Prefatory Note" and concluding "Editorial Note" which supply useful background information; but it omits the author's footnotes and concentrates his forty brief chapters into nineteen longer ones conventionally titled from "The Early Years" to "The End of the Road." These changes may enhance the book for readers who approach it as a political chronicle of the times, and at least one reviewer whose orientation is political preferred this abridged version.[15] But to the extent that it molds the biography into a chronicle, the abridgment detracts from its artistic effectiveness.

Even the decision to omit footnotes was taken at some cost to the integrity of the text. For example, Paton is concerned with the extent to which Hofmeyr's liberal views contributed to the disintegration of the United Party. He quotes the view of Judge Leslie Blackwell that Hofmeyr's famous speech in 1936 opposing the curtailment of African voting rights precipitated the party split. Paton introduces this quotation with the statement, "It is interesting to read what Blackwell wrote about what he called 'this mem-

orable speech.' " Judge Blackwell, as a distinguished national figure and as a friend of the Hofmeyr family, plays a role in the
biography. His opinion on this important point bears greater
weight than any anonymous opinion, yet, apparently to avoid a
footnote reference to the source of the quotation, the text is
changed to "It is interesting to read what one publicist
wrote . . ." The change is not only unnecessary, but meaningless,
because what makes the quoted opinion *interesting* is that it was
Blackwell's opinion. Again, for the sake of omitting the words
"Mr. B. J. Vorster, in 1962," it seems hardly worth witholding the
information that the author of the axiom, "Communism kills, but
Liberalism leads one into ambush in order to kill," is the present
Prime Minister of South Africa.

An abridgment must necessarily condense a text or omit portions of it. While, in general, this abridgment succeeds in its aim
of presenting the substance of the biography in clear readable
form, it unfortunately omits some details essential to the complete
characterization of the man. For example, the account earlier in
this chapter of Paton's interest in the drama of a man's attempt to
balance principle and expediency relies for a concrete instance on
Hofmeyr's public and private disbursments on African education.
The abridgment completely omits the account of the Trust Fund
through which Hofmeyr donated four-fifths of his salary to African education. This deprives the reader of a significant insight
into Hofmeyr's character and diminishes the inner drama on
which the biography depends so much for its impact.

There can be no doubt that Paton saw the inner drama as of
paramount importance. The internal evidence from his account of
Hofmeyr's own immature essay in biography has already been
cited. After completing the work Paton wrote an essay on his experience. In it he speaks of Hofmeyr's career as a subject for biography and comments: "As if these things were not enough for a
biographic symphony, there were the two extraordinary relationships, not fully explicated because not fully explicable, of himself
and his mother, and himself and Smuts. If such a symphony
turned out to be dull, it would be only the composer who was to
blame." [16] In *Hofmeyr*, Paton succeeds to a very high degree in
attaining the completeness of a symphony. The abridgment necessarily deprives the conductor of a tympanist here and a viola
there.

Paton has written only one biography and he disclaims expertness in the medium. He says: "It is an experience not easily paralleled to write a man's life. You live with him for years. You share his hopes and his despair—and Hofmeyr came sometimes near to despair." As for his biographical method, his own description is, again, the most appropriate:

Then you take it all, the chronology, the letters, the interviews, your own knowledge, Hansard [i.e., the parliamentary record], the newspaper cuttings, the history books, the diary, the thousand hours of contemplation, and you try to make a whole of it, not a chronicle but a drama, with a beginning and an end, the whole being given form and integrity because a man moves through it from birth to death, through all the beauty and terror of human life.[17]

As a literary achievement Paton's *Hofmeyr* has no rival among South African biographies. Sir Keith Hancock's two volume biography, *Smuts*, is a fine scholarly, rather than literary, achievement; and Sarah Gertrude Millin's two-volume *General Smuts* (1936), was completed fifteen years before Smuts died, and necessarily lacks the wholeness and unity that Paton's *Hofmeyr* achieves. Judged as a work of scholarship, Paton's biography has deficiencies. He is not meticulous about supplying exact references for source material, and he is over careful in avoiding references to himself. His own name does not even appear in the index —although this may be a simple oversight. As a literary biography, however, it merits comparison with the best works in this genre; as one reviewer put it, "it is entirely possible that Paton's life of Hofmeyr will be shelved among classic biographies." [18]

CHAPTER 8

Race and Reason: The Long View

I The Liberal Party

WHEN Paton made up his mind in 1952 to work no longer on his biography of Jan Hofmeyr while Mrs. Hofmeyr lived, he was for a time uncertain of his future course. Feeling at a crossroads, and troubled by the spate of new laws and regulations designed to perpetuate *apartheid,* he decided to devote a year or more to working in a tuberculosis settlement for Africans at Botha's Hill, Natal. Botha's Hill was then a new project with only two buildings on a thirty-acre site. While there, Paton intended to work with his hands, as he had frequently done at Diepkloof, to help build sufficient accommodations for 600 people. In response to an inquiry from the *Saturday Review,* he wrote in August, 1953: "At the moment my wife and I are at the Toc-H TB Settlement at Botha's Hill. The task of the settlement is to help Africans who have had TB to return to normal life. We have given ourselves to this work for a year and are enjoying it." He goes on to say, "We are also working for the new Liberal Party, whose aim is to accustom South Africa to the idea that our only hope is to open the doors of our society to all people who are ready for it, no matter what their race or colour." [1]

While at Botha's Hill, Paton wrote *South Africa and Her People,* a volume in the Portraits of the Nations series designed for high school students in Britain and America. In the United States it was published under the title *The Land and People of South Africa.* Paton presents South Africa to his young readers in the guise of a conducted tour. He avoids controversial issues during the course of the "tour," and saves his estimate of the present situation in South Africa for a closing chapter that looks toward the future. *The Land and People of South Africa* is illustrated by photographs of notable excellence. These are a selection from the book *South Africa in Transition,* a striking visual record of South Africa, and of her African people in particular, compiled by Paton and the American photographer Dan Weiner. Weiner's photographs constitute the bulk of this volume. They corroborate Paton's views on the inherent dignity of all human beings—of whatever race or status—to a remarkable degree, for every photograph captures a vital, vibrant human personality.

Neither *The Land and People of South Africa* nor *South Africa in Transition* is the kind of book Paton had in mind when he retired from Diepkloof to devote himself to interpreting South Africa. While each of these books has its own particular merit, it is the merit of good journalism and not of original creativity—of a competent writer marking time in a period of uncertainty. It was not that Paton was uncertain about where he stood or what he believed; but he was reluctant to enter public life, and uncertain therefore about what role he could play.

Despite his natural disinclination, Paton firmly took the step of entering public life in 1956 when he accepted the national Chairmanship of the new South African Liberal Party. The question of establishing a Liberal Party was frequently discussed in some circles in South Africa, and Paton's *Hofmeyr* traces the history of this issue which was unresolved in Hofmeyr's lifetime. The decision to found a Liberal Party was taken after the elections of 1953 at a meeting of the South African Liberal Association, which had previously supported the United Party. A policy statement issuing from this meeting declared that the newly-founded Liberal Party recognized the essential dignity of every human being without regard for race, color, or creed. It also declared that the Liberal Party was opposed to all forms of totalitarianism such as Communism or Fascism, and that it rejected racial bars to participation in government.

This meeting of the Liberal Association elected the new Party's first slate of officers: Mrs. Margaret Ballinger, then a member of parliament representing Africans, as President; Leo Marquard and Alan Paton as Vice-Presidents; Dr. Oscar Wolheim as National Chairman; and Leslie Rubin as Vice-Chairman. Since the main organizational tasks fell to Oscar Wolheim and Leslie Rubin, Paton's post as Vice-President, while not quite honorary, did not engage him in daily active work on behalf of the party. He continued to write serious commentaries on racial and religious questions that were not immediately pertinent to the work of the Liberal Party. He undertook, for example, an extensive tour of the

United States in 1954, at the invitation of *Collier's*, to report on race relations in America; and he set down his views in two articles: "The Negro in America Today," and "The Negro in the North." [2] During this tour he also addressed the World Council of Churches meeting at Evanston, Illinois, and visited Yale University to receive the honorary degree of Doctor of Humane Letters.

Paton returned to the United States in 1956 while Robert Yale Libott's dramatized version of *Too Late the Phalarope* was being prepared for the Broadway stage. This play opened its Broadway run at the Belasco Theater on October 11, 1956, with Barry Sullivan as Pieter van Vlaanderen, and the Scottish actor Finlay Currie as Jakob. Reviews of the play are surprisingly similar to some of the reviews of *Sponono* eight years later—lamenting the lack of public interest in drama with a serious theme. John Gassner remarks in his *Theatre at the Crossroads* that "the work earned respect for everyone associated with it. But *Too Late the Phalarope* could not win its bout with the Broadway public." [3]

Back in South Africa, however, a drama was taking place on the national scene calculated to diminish Paton's interest in the problems of drama on Broadway. After his election as National Chairman, Paton undertook the duty of organizing the Liberal Party purposefully. He also continued to write, but now much of what he wrote was directly concerned with the policies and aims of the Liberal Party—as is the case with such books and pamphlets as *Hope for South Africa, The People Wept,* and *The Charlestown Story.* But one of the tasks that he undertook in 1956 that was to remain with him as a source of concern for ten years, was an unexpected one arising from the dramatic South African Treason Trial that began in December, 1956, and continued for four years.

On December 5, 1956, South Africans of all races were arrested and charged with treason under the Suppression of Communism Act. Those arrested included such African leaders as Chief Albert Luthuli, subsequently a recipient of the Nobel Peace Prize, and Professor Z. K. Matthews, a highly respected educator. On the day after these arrests, Paton, together with Bishop Reeves of Johannesburg, Dr. Ellen Hellman of the Institute of Race Relations, Alex Hepple, a Labor Party member of parliament, and Judge Frank Lucas, organized the Treason Trial Defence Fund to enable those accused of treason to have adequate defense.

No one could then foresee how long and how costly the Treason

Trial was to be. During the four years that the trial lasted, the Defence Fund collected several hundred thousand dollars for legal expenses, and also to provide some aid for the dependents of those detained. When the verdict was finally given on March 29, 1961, all the accused were acquitted, but the organizers of the Defence Fund were not able to close the books on their undertakeing. As a consequence of the State of Emergency declared in South Africa in 1960, many people were arrested and detained under the administration's emergency powers. To draw attention to the numbers imprisoned, Paton with Mrs. Albert Luthuli, Fatima Meer, and Manilal Gandhi's widow led night-long fasting and prayers—in which they were joined by hundreds of Africans and Indians on May 31, 1960, the day on which fifty years of Union was being celebrated in South Africa.[4] To assist those in prison, the fund organized for the Treason Trial was broadened in purpose in 1960, and re-named the Defence and Aid Fund. It established regional offices and published a quarterly newsletter called D and A.

Defence and Aid was soon attacked as a subversive organization, and those associated with it were denounced by some newspapers as "Catspaws of the Communists" and as "fellow-travelers." During 1965, opposition to the fund intensified, particularly when the government of Holland donated $28,000 to it. In answering critics of Defence and Aid, Paton pointed out that even those presumed guilty had the right to adequate legal representation, and that unless this right was conceded, the administration of justice itself was in danger of erosion: "It is to me a duty owing not only to the accused person, not only to the judge, but supremely to our society, that adequate defence should be secured in a society where passions are so intense, and where many white South Africans regard security as far more important than justice."[5] But Defence and Aid was, nevertheless, banned under the terms of the all-purpose Suppression of Communism Act. The ban was announced at midnight on March 20, 1966. Early next morning the security police raided regional offices and the homes of some Committee members. They visited Paton's home that morning, too, and took away papers related to the fund.

During the early years of Paton's Chairmanship, before intense opposition and restrictions devitalized it, the spirit of the Liberal Party was good. As a non-racial party it had very little support among the white population (and only the white population enjoyed the right to vote), but its members were convinced that their philosophy of a common society offered the only real alternative to rigid racial separation, and they were prepared to present their case to the voters. They therefore entered candidates for both local and national office in the election campaigns of 1958, and established a lively journal of opinion called *Contact* to put their views before the public.

This confident spirit pervades Paton's *Hope for South Africa* (1958), which is a clear exposition of the Liberal Party's purpose and philosophy unadorned by political rhetoric or special pleading. This book begins with an account of the meaning of the term *liberal* in South Africa, where the word has connotations unparalleled elsewhere, except perhaps in Alabama or the Kremlin. In South Africa a supporter of liberal policies is frequently described as a *liberalist*—a term that carries overtones of immoral behavior and dubious patriotism. The dominant Nationalist Party envisions no political spectrum, but only two irreconcilable extremes—nationalism and liberalism.

Paton's *Hope for South Africa* has four chapters on the history of South Africa and the rise of the Afrikaner that provide the background for present day attitudes to the liberal approach to race relations. The rest of *Hope for South Africa* reviews the role of the Liberal Party in and out of Parliament in its attempt "to influence the progress of South Africa from a white-dominated state to a non-racial democracy." At the time that Paton wrote *Hope for South Africa* there were two Liberal Party members in Parliament—the African representatives, Mrs. Margaret Ballinger and Donald Molteno. Since this representation was abolished in 1960 there have been none; and by 1966 the brave hopes of 1958 for a Liberal Party role in Parliament were no longer tenable. J. B. Vorster, the South African Minister for Justice, now Prime Minister, took seriously his own axiom, "Communism kills, but Liberalism leads one into an ambush in order to kill." He used his Emergency powers to shackle the Liberal Party by banning many of its leading members from political or other public activity.

II Contact *and* The Long View

Paton was one of the board of directors of *Contact*, the journal of opinion launched in 1958 to put the Liberal Party's views be-

fore the public. *Contact* has shared the hopes and frustrations of
the Liberal Party to such an extent that even the external appearance of a run of this magazine assembled on library shelves
mutely illustrates the fortunes of the Liberal Party. A glance at
the file will show that *Contact* began in February, 1958, as a well-
designed magazine comparable in appearance to any journal produced by a competent professional staff. At first it appeared every
two weeks, and had, well-printed, illustrated, 14½ by 11 inch
pages. For the first year or two it attracted a substantial amount
of advertising, including that of major national business concerns
such as oil and tobacco companies.

But the copies of *Contact* from 1960 to 1963 no longer proclaim
it to be a successfully produced news magazine. They vary
abruptly in size, and noticeably lack advertising—particularly
that of national business concerns. There are fewer issues on the
shelves, too, for *Contact* has changed from a brave fortnightly
magazine to a monthly newspaper "For United Non-Racial Action." The issue for August, 1964, is mimeographed, with this ex-
planation of a "temporary change" by the editors:

Since 1960 this newspaper has endured most of the penalties
heaped on those who speak out openly and in clear opposition in a
police state. It has suffered the disruption of police searches and of
several prosecutions; it has had two editors and other members of its
staff banned; its selling agents have been repeatedly harassed; and
three or four times it has had to change its printers. The last change
was made, unfortunately, with very little notice and came too late for
suitable alternative printing arrangements to bring the newspaper out
before the end of August.

To this the editors add the brave assertion:

. . . we shall continue to publish as long as we have one person with
one typewriter and one machine left to print or duplicate what we
believe must be said from inside South Africa.[6]

Contact continued to keep up its registration as a newspaper
and to appear monthly in a variety of printed forms. By July,
1965, five editors and six staff members and contributors had been
served banning orders. More than thirty-five printers, fearing the
consequences to themselves, had refused to print the paper, and

the staff was forced to do the job. By late 1965 *Contact* was reduced to a few folded mimeographed sheets and it finally gave up
its registration as a newspaper; in 1966 it no longer appeared in
monthly issues, but only from time to time. All other radical newspapers in South Africa had by this time "collapsed of their own
accord"; even the highly reputable *Forum*, the journal of liberal
opinion founded in 1938 to promote Jan Hofmeyr's philosophy,
had ceased publication for lack of support. *Contact*, nevertheless,
kept its promise to continue publishing "as long as we have one
person with one typewriter and one machine left to print or duplicate what we believe must be said." By 1966 *Contact* had, in fact,
little more than one typewriter in its office. The office had been
raided at times not only by the police, but also by thugs who
removed or destroyed equipment; even the office telephone was
given up to avoid the frequent interruption of threatening telephone calls.

The significance of this sketch of the history of *Contact* in an
account of the writings of Alan Paton is this: not once, even during *Contact's* worst trials, did Paton fail to produce his regular
column, "The Long View." Paton wrote three series for this column: the first during 1958, the second during 1960, and the third
from 1964 to the present; since the second half of 1965, each issue
of *Contact* has consisted mainly of Paton's column, together with
brief accounts of judicial bannings culled from other newspapers.
Paton's regular contributions demonstrate his determination to
stand behind *Contact's* non-racial program. But from the literary
viewpoint, his contributions to *Contact* have added significance
because they constitute a substantial portion of the creative work
of a writer who has thought deeply about the dangers of racism—
not only for South Africa but for the world at large in the twentieth century.

Paton's essays in *Contact* have been collected for publication in
the United States under the title *The Long View*. The immediate
subject matter of these essays is the political ideal of *apartheid,* or
separate development of racial groups, constituting the social ide-
ology of Afrikaner nationalism which Paton has described as "the
most perfect blend of idealism and cruelty ever devised by man."
This immediate subject is not, however, treated in isolation, but
rather as one manifestation of the universal dilemma of our times
—the dilemma of individual persons living in the present, yet con-

fronted with political systems determined to mold their lives to some ideal based on exclusive purity of race or class, and promising a perfect state at some time in the future.

III *1960: State of Emergency and Freedom Award*

In 1959 Paton gave up the Chairmanship of the Liberal Party to return to work on his biography of Jan Hofmeyr. He was given the specially-created post of President of the Liberal Party and he was succeeded as Chairman by Peter Brown, who took over his active duties, including the column "The Long View" for *Contact*. But his work on the biography was interrupted by the State of Emergency declared in South Africa following the events at Sharpeville in March, 1960. In the early morning of March 30, 1960, the police detained 234 men and women of all races, among them Peter Brown. Brown was kept in prison without trial for four months, and Paton once again undertook the active duties of Chairman of the Liberal Party: "At real personal risk and cost, he ran the national office of the Party and led the Party in all ways." [7]

Paton wrote his second series of essays for "The Long View" in *Contact* while replacing Peter Brown during this Emergency period. His task was now doubly difficult; not only were the tensions within South Africa extreme, but some supporters of the Liberal Party's non-racial policies were discouraged by the violence in the Congo. They were discouraged, in particular, by the racist aspects of this violence, and by Mr. Lumumba's demands that *white* United Nations troops be withdrawn. Paton did not evade these sensitive subjects in his new series, but addressed himself to them courageously.

In the midst of the tensions and pressures of the State of Emergency, supporters of the Liberal Party were heartened by Paton's nomination for the 1960 Freedom Award. The Freedom Award has been conferred annually since 1943 by Freedom House, New York, on outstanding defenders of civil liberties and the ideals of democracy. Freedom House, New York—headquarters of several associated organizations—was so named to symbolize opposition to what Hitler's Braunhaus in Munich stood for; since World War II it has worked to oppose totalitarian systems of both the Fascist and Communist varieties, and to further justice and individual freedoms. Earlier recipients of the annual Freedom Award include

Sir Winston Churchill, Franklin Roosevelt, Dwight Eisenhower, George C. Marshall, and Dag Hammarskjold.

In preparing to nominate the recipient of its annual Award, Freedom House first defines the dominating issue currently affecting freedom, and then decides who best symbolizes the struggle in that area. In the late fifties its members emphasized the issue of race relations in the United States; in 1960 they defined worldwide racism to be the prevailing issue: "And among the fighters for freedom one name stood out—a citizen of South Africa, a brilliant novelist with a tender heart and tough mind . . . Alan Paton was the logical choice for the Freedom Award of 1960." [8]

Paton came to New York to receive the Award at the annual Freedom House ceremony honoring recipients on October 5, 1960. His presence aroused great interest, and "representatives of the literary and political worlds came in such numbers that many had to be turned away." President Eisenhower sent a message of congratulations which read, in part, "Through his brave and sensitive writings on behalf of the underprivileged, Mr. Paton has worked to remove the social and racial barriers which plague mankind. In striving to achieve for all men recognition of the dignity to which they are entitled, he stands as a fine symbol of Freedom House."

Archibald MacLeish, who presented the Award, characterized Paton as follows:

To live at the center of the contemporary maelstrom; to see it for what it is and to challenge the passions of those who struggle in it beside him with the voice of reason—with, if he will forgive me, the enduring reasons of love; to offer the quiet sanity of the heart in a city yammering with the crazy slogans of fear; to do all this at the cost of tranquility and the risk of harm, as a service to a government which does not know it needs it . . . is to deserve far more of history than we can give our guest tonight.

In some remarks preliminary to his address accepting the award, Paton said that although he did not feel worthy of it, he could not have refused it, "for the very announcement of it brought hope and encouragement to thousands of my fellow citizens in South Africa." And he went on: "Though you give this award to me, I feel, and many of them feel, that you are giving it to them. Many of them have had to pay for their beliefs and

principles more dearly than I have been called upon to do; some
of them spent a considerable part of this year in prison, arrested,
detained and released without preferring any charge against
them." [9]

Apart from these opening remarks, Paton made no further reference to events in South Africa. He devoted the body of his address, in which he spoke as an African rather than as a South
African, to the problems of the African continent emerging from
colonial rule, to race attitudes, and to the relations of the new
African states to Western countries on the one hand, and to Communist states on the other. He pointed to three striking characteristics of the new Africa: the desire and determination to have
freedom; the desire to walk as equals among the nations of the
modern world; the bitter resentment against the arrogance of the
color-bar that expresses itself in its extreme form as anti-Western-
ism.

In the course of his return journey to South Africa, Paton addressed some meetings in England to help raise money for Defence and Aid. He also attended the World Council of Churches
meetings in Geneva, Switzerland. When he arrived at Johannesburg airport his passport was confiscated by government officials.
An editorial in the *New York Times* hailed this act as "A New
Honor for Alan Paton." The government-run South African
Broadcasting Corporation bitterly attacked him for being unpatriotic, but refused to allow him to reply on its transmitters. Responding through the press, Paton said that he did not identify
the Nationalists with South Africa, and that he did not regard it as
unpatriotic to criticize them abroad. He interpreted the summary
withdrawal of his passport as the penalty imposed by the Nationalists after twelve years in power for having continued to say
and write what he thought to be the truth. He was equally unre-
pentant in a letter to the cabinet minister who had ordered his
passport withdrawn. He wrote: "I hope to have my passport returned in due course by a government fully representative of the
people of South Africa." [10]

IV *Freedom's Advocate*

Looking back over Alan Paton's creative endeavors in the cause
of human welfare as well as in the craft of fiction, one comes to
realize the appropriateness of the Freedom Award as a recogni-

tion of his distinction. Freedom has been his consistent touchstone. As a guardian of delinquent boys he put his faith in freedom as the supreme instrument of reform, and he took advantage of every occasion offered him, in speech or in writing, to propagate his belief in the primacy of freedom. The members of Freedom House rightly recognized his championship of freedom in the civil sphere; but to grasp fully the philosophy underlying his literary works one must recognize that Paton, in a sense, also sees freedom as the supreme Christian virtue. He does not substitute freedom for love, the primal virtue laid down in the admonition. "Thou shall love thy neighbor as thyself"; he equates love and freedom. Therefore, in *Cry, the Beloved Country,* love, or the recognition of human brotherhood, is the catalyst that dissolves the hate secreted by fear. Love frees from fear; freedom from fear in turn permits the personality to express itself creatively and so to realize its fullest potential.

Since attention has already been drawn to an article by Paton that treats the social themes of his first novel (in Chapter 3, above), it may be appropriate here to introduce another article which bears equally close relation to the religious implications of all his fiction. This is the philosophical essay, "The Unrecognized Power," that first appeared in the *Saturday Review* and has since been reprinted more than once under the title "Religious Faith and Human Brotherhood." This essay is written from the point of view of a Christian who cherishes the ideal of brotherhood and of the oneness of the human race. In psychological terms it sets the desire to dominate over against the impulse toward human brotherhood; that is to say, it presents the desire to dominate as the exact opposite of the intention of the admonition "Love thy neighbor."

The highest inner law of human nature, Paton implies, is analogous to the command "Love thy neighbor," because the inner law tends to venerate "something that resides in the creature which we may call personality and which expresses itself in creativity." This veneration for personality must be applied to oneself as well as to others. One may not, therefore, "in the belief that it is Christian humility, consent to any violation of one's own personality by others." Recognition of this fundamental concept will help clarify many of Paton's statements on the necessity for opposing laws that debase human personality.

As Christian humility does not imply debasement of the self, so proper human pride does not imply arrogance, which is the mark of the desire to dominate. Paton says that "the really evil thing about Hitlerism . . . was that it committed unspeakable crimes against personality." And he adds, "It is not strange, therefore, that one of the chief qualities of its disciples was arrogance, nor that the desire to dominate should come to be regarded as some gift of Providence . . ." It is, of course, to this arrogant pride of race that Tante Sophie refers in *Too Late the Phalarope* when she says, "I pray that we shall not walk arrogant, remembering Herod whom an Angel of the Lord struck down."

In "The Unrecognized Power," Paton describes the post-war drive of Asian and African nations for independence as a massive revolt against domination and, therefore, as an expression of the inner personal drive for creative freedom. Those with vested intrests fear this creative drive and resist it. In this fearfulness, he says, reason is dethroned in favor of what the baser emotions dictate. Here, on the international plane, he would go forward with Hofmeyr in faith, not fear, toward freedom as an instrument of peace: "Just as we have freed our children," he says, "because we loved them and thereby conquered our fears, just so we can free the world, and release for the good of all humanity the gifts and energies of its people." [11]

Paton has undertaken various tasks in the course of his career so far. He has been a teacher, a penal reformer, a writer, and a politician. But his various interests are not unrelated segments; they constitute a whole centered on his regard for the inherent dignity of persons and his faith in the power of freedom to emancipate men from the bonds of ignorance, and the shackles of their own fears. In the political sphere it is true that his ideas have met only with reverses and no practical success. It is, of course, painful to him to suffer reverses and to see many supporters of the Liberal Party banned or imprisoned; yet he responds with such articles as "Beware of Melancholy." [12] Darkness is, after all, inevitably followed by dawn, as the close of *Cry, the Beloved Country* reminds us: "For it is the dawn that has come, as it has come for a thousand centuries never failing. But when the dawn will come, of our emancipation, from the fear of bondage and the bondage of fear, why, that is a secret."

Notes and References

1. *Lost in the Stars,* a musical tragedy, with book by Maxwell Anderson; music by Kurt Weill; based on Alan Paton's novel, *Cry, the Beloved Country;* staged by Rouben Mamoulian; presented by the Playwrights Company at the Music Box Theatre, New York. The play opened on October 30, 1949, and continued for 273 performances. Revived as an opera by the New York City Opera Company during the 1950 Spring season. Text: Maxwell Anderson, *Lost in the Stars* (New York, 1950), 86 pp.

2. *Cry, the Beloved Country,* London Films, 1951. Directed by Zoltan Korda. Filmed partly in South African settings. Canada Lee as Stephen Kumalo; Sidney Poitier as Msimangu. U.S. distribution by Lopert. Rental: Audio Film Center, 2138 East 75th Street, Chicago.

3. *Cry, the Beloved Country: A Verse Drama;* adapted from Alan Paton's novel by Felicia Komai (b. 1926) with the collaboration of Josephine Douglas. First produced in the chruch of St. Martin-in-the-Fields, London, February, 1954. First published, London: Edinburgh House, 1954, 80 pp.; New York: Friendship Press, 1955.

4. Translations of *Cry, the Beloved Country* soon appeared in many countries including Norway, Sweden, Denmark, The Netherlands, Finland, Czechoslovakia, France, Italy, Israel, Japan, Greece, Yugoslavia, Spain, and Portugal. In South Africa it was translated into Afrikaans and Zulu, in India into Hindi, and in Iran into Persian.

5. "Church, State and Race," *Christian Century,* LXXV (February 26, 1958), 248.

6. "The Road," *New Yorker,* XXVI (December 17, 1960), 32.

7. *The Land and People of South Africa* (New York, 1955), pp. 80–81.

8. *Contact,* III (No. 17, August 27, 1960), 6.

9. *South Africa Today* (New York, 1951), p. 31.

10. John K. Hutchins, "Alan Paton," *New York Herald Tribune Book Review* (November 6, 1949), 2.

11. The National Union of South African Students invited Senator

Robert Kennedy to South Africa in May, 1966. He met Paton at a luncheon in Durban.

12. *Natal University College Magazine*, III (November, 1920), 8.

13. *Ibid.*, VI (June, 1922), 19–20.

14. *Ibid.*, IV (June, 1921), 48–49.

15. *Ibid.*, V (November, 1921), 10–11.

16. *Ibid.*, VII (1922), 34–35.

17. *Ibid.*, IX (October, 1923), 26. The final line originally concluded, "'I have come,' He said." Version quoted here supplied by Alan Paton.

18. *Ibid.*

19. "The Imperial Conference," *Natal University College Magazine*, XI (October, 1924), 9–12. Source of all subsequent references to the Conference.

20. That Ixopo High School served white students is emphasized here because many sources rely on misleading text and photographs in *Life* (November, 1949), pp. 142–143, showing Paton with Zulu children at a small mission school at Ixopo "like the one . . . where he used to teach."

21. "Tragic and Lovely Land of South Africa," *Holiday*, XXI (February, 1957), 34.

22. *Natal University College Magazine*, Commemoration Number (1934), 37–39.

23. "The Prevention of Crime," *Race Relations*, XII (1945), 72.

24. *Salute to My Greatgrandchildren* (Johannesburg, 1952), p. 10.

25. "Jan Hendrick Hofmeyr—An Appreciation," *South African Opinion*, September 18, 1936, pp. 6–7. ("Signed M. P. to give the impression of inside knowledge, but in fact the letters stood for Mr. Paton"—see *Hofmeyr*, p. 236 n.).

26. Letter to E. C., April, 1966.

CHAPTER TWO

1. Letter to E. C., April, 1966.

2. Remarks by Mr. Alan Paton in "Minutes of a Conference On Urban Juvenile Native Delinquency Held at Johannesburg," October, 1938, pp. 10–12. (From the files of the South African Institute of Race Relations).

3. Guy Butler (ed.), *A Book of South African Verse* (London, 1959), p. 72.

4. "Minutes of a Conference . . .", see n. 2 above.

5. "Juvenile Delinquency and Its Treatment," *Community and Crime* (Pretoria, 1949), p. 53.

6. *Hofmeyr*, (Cape Town, 1964), p. 274; *South African Tragedy* (New York, 1965), p. 211.

7. "Let's Build Model Prisons," *Forum*, VII (May 27, 1944), 24.

8. W. H. Auden, "The Poet and the City," *The Dyer's Hand* (New York, 1962), p. 84.

9. *Hofmeyr*, p. 293; *South African Tragedy*, p. 228.

10. *Forum*, I (September, 1938), quoted in *Hofmeyr*, pp. 294–295.

11. "The Real Way to Cure Crime," *Forum*, IV (January 29, 1944), 24.

12. *Ibid.*

13. *Hofmeyr*, p. 164; *South African Tragedy*, p. 117.

14. *Hofmeyr*, p. 244; *South African Tragedy*, p. 193.

15. "A Deep Experience," *Contrast*, I (December, 1961), 23–24; reprinted in *The Long View* (New York, 1967); also the source of quotations in the paragraph following.

16. *Freedom as a Reformatory Instrument* (Pretoria, 1948), pp. 3–4. During this tour Paton, while in England, attended a conference of Christians and Jews at Oxford and wrote an account of it for *The Outspan* (South Africa), XL (September 13, 1946), 34–35.

CHAPTER THREE

1. *Forum*, VIII (December 15, 1945), 7–8; source of quotations in the three paragraphs following.

2. Horton Davies, "Alan Paton: Literary Artist and Anglican," *The Hibbert Journal*, I (April 1952), 266.

3. Hoernlé's writings: R. F. A. Hoernlé, *South African Native Policy and the Liberal Spirit* (Cape Town, 1939); *Race and Reason*, ed. with a memoir by J. D. MacCrone (Johannesburg, 1945).

4. J. M. Synge, Preface to *The Playboy of the Western World*; Alan Paton, interview with John K. Hutchens; *New York Herald Tribune Book Review* (November 6, 1949), p. 2.

5. Although Jarvis reads it, the Gettysburg Address is not quoted in the novel.

CHAPTER FOUR

1. Austin Roberts, *The Birds of South Africa* (6th ed.; Johannesburg, 1948); revised by A. McLaughlin and R. Liversidge (Johannesburg, 1957). Phalarope: plover or snipe-like birds that "swim more than other waders and often seek their food far from land on the surface of the water" (Roberts, *The Birds of South Africa*, 5th ed., 1940).

2. L. C. Bekker and G. J. Potgieter, *Voorligting vir Standerd* VIII, (Johannesburg, 1960), 48 ff. Quotation translated by Edward Callan.

3. "The South African Novel in English," *Report of the Proceedings*

of a Conference of Writers . . . Held at the University of the Wit-watersrand, July 10–12, 1956 (Johannesburg, 1957), p. 150.

4. Paton may have hit on the device of the diary after his own un-expected discovery of a personal diary among Jan Hofmeyr's papers—"But the big discovery was the diary . . . without this corroboration many people would have rejected the closing chapters of the biog-raphy"—"The Hofmeyr Biography," *Contrast,* X (October, 1964), 33.

CHAPTER FIVE

1. *Tales from a Troubled Land* (New York, 1961); *Debbie Go Home,* (London, 1961). For dates of individual publication of these stories see the appended bibliography.

2. "The South African Novel in English," p. 151.

3. "The Trial," *Contact,* IX (April, 1966), 7.

4. "The Novelist and Christ" (with Liston Pope), *Saturday Review,* XXVII (December 4, 1954), 15–16.

5. Lewis Nkosi, *Home and Exile* (London, 1965).

6. Trevor Huddleston, *Naught For Your Comfort* (New York, 1956), p. 80.

7. "A Personal View," *New York Times,* March 29, 1964, Sec. 2, p. 1.

8. "The Prevention of Crime," *Race Relations,* XII, No. 3 (1945), 42.

9. "Four Splendid Voices," introduction by Alan Paton to *Quartet: New Voices from South Africa,* edited by Richard Rive (New York: Crown Publishers, Inc., 1963). Copyright 1963 by Crown Publishers, Inc. Used by permission of Crown Publishers, Inc.

CHAPTER SIX

1. "Nationalism and the Theatre," *Contact,* VIII (March, 1965), 2–3; reprinted in *The Long View.*

2. "Author's Note," substantially reproduced in H. Fosbrooke, "Play Review: *The Last Journey* by Alan Paton," *Northern Rhodesia Journal,* IV, No. 1 (1959), 97–99.

3. *Ibid.,* p. 98.

4. Letter to E. C., August, 1966.

5. *Sponono* by Alan Paton and Krishna Shah. Staged by Krishna Shah. Presented by Mary K. Frank. Traditional chants arranged by Gideon Nxumalo. Presented at the Cort Theater, New York, for twenty performances: Thursday, April 2, 1964, to Saturday, April 18, 1964. Krishna Shah is best known in the United States for his direction of Tagore's *King of the Dark Chambers* which ran for 255 performances.

6. *New York Times,* April 3, 1964, p. 28.

7. *Intermission,* II No. 29 (March 6, 1966), 3. *Intermission Magazine* is published by Hull House Theater, Chicago, Illinois.

8. *New York Times,* April 3, 1964, p. 28.

9. "Play of the Month," *The Catholic World,* CXCIX (June 1964), 199–200.

10. *Sponono,* directed by Michael Miller, Parkway Community Theater, Chicago. Opened Friday, February 25, 1966, for ten weekends.

11. *Chicago Daily News,* February 28, 1966, p. 32.

12. Guy Butler (ed.), *A Book of South African Verse* (London, 1959).

13. "Apartheid," *South African Outlook,* LXXXIII (January, 1953), 16.

14. *Africa South,* I (April-June, 1957), 94–97.

15. (London, 1959).

16. *Forum* (February 26, 1949); reprinted in *Hofmeyr* and *South African Tragedy.*

17. *Contrast,* I (No. 4, 1961), 17.

CHAPTER SEVEN

1. "Jan Hendrik Hofmeyr: An Appreciation," *South African Opinion* (September 18, 1936), 7, 12. "It was signed M. P. to give the impression of inside knowledge, but in fact the letters stood for Mr. Paton" (Paton, *Hofmeyr,* p. 236). This is not the journal *South African Opinion* published during 1944–1947, but an earlier journal of the same name.

2. "The Hofmeyr Biography," *Contrast,* III, No. 2 (October, 1964), 32–36.

3. Preface to *The Little Karoo* by Pauline Smith (London, 1950).

4. Extract quoted in Horton Davies, "Alan Paton: Literary Artist and Anglican," *The Hibbert Journal,* I (April, 1952), 263.

5. "The Hofmeyr Biography" (note 2, above), source of quotation in preceding paragraph.

6. "South African Story," *Times Literary Supplement,* April 29, 1965, p. 328.

7. *The Dyer's Hand* (New York, 1962), p. 81.

8. "The Hofmeyr Biography" (note 2, above).

9. *Forum,* I (September 26, 1938). Quoted in *Hofmeyr,* pp. 294–295.

10. Quoted from Tom MacDonald, *Jan Hofmeyr: Heir to Smuts* (London, 1948), pp. 12–13. Paton discusses this speech in *Hofmeyr,* pp. 421–23; *South African Tragedy,* pp. 325–327.

11. *Perspective on Ideas and the Arts* (Gale Broadcasting Company, Chicago), XII (May, 1963), 29.

12. Italicized quotation shows identical wording from "A Deep Experience" and *Hofmeyr*, p. 173; *South African Tragedy*, p. 125.

13. Interview with Studs Terkel, *Perspective*, XII (May, 1963), 29.

14. "The Hofmeyr Biography" (note 2, above), p. 35.

15. Ronald Segal, *Book Week*, (November 14, 1965), p. 2.

16. "The Hofmeyr Biography," p. 33.

17. *Ibid.*, p. 36.

18. Edward Callan, "A Light Went Out," *New York Times Book Review*, (November 21, 1965), 44.

CHAPTER EIGHT

1. *Saturday Review*, XXVI (August 22, 1953), 10.

2. *Collier's*, CXXXIV (October 15, 1954), 20, 52–56; and CXXXIV (October 29, 1954), 70–80.

3. John Gassner, *"Too Late the Phalarope*: Alternatives in Social Drama," *Theatre at the Crossroads* (New York, 1960), pp. 177–180.

4. Mary Benson, *The African Patriots* (New York, 1964), p. 274. For Paton's views on the Treason Trial and a more complete description of the Defence Fund, see his articles on the trial in *New Republic* (November, 1957) and *Atlantic* (January, 1960).

5. "Defence and Aid," *Contact*, VIII (June, 1965), 2; reprinted in *The Long View* (New York, 1967).

6. *Contact*, VII (August, 1964), 1.

7. *Contact*, III (August 27, 1960), 6.

8. Aaron Levenstein and William Agar, *Freedom's Advocate* (New York, 1965), p. 153. Also the source of quoted material in the next two paragraphs, including remarks by President Eisenhower and Archibald MacLeish.

9. Alan Paton, Freedom Award Address, 1960. Included in *The Long View*.

10. *Contact*, III (December 17, 1960), 2.

11. Quotations in this and preceding paragraphs from Alan Paton, "Religious Faith and Human Brotherhood" in A. William Loos (ed.), *Religious Faith and World Culture* (New York, 1951), pp. 189–199.

12. *Contact*, VIII (July 1965). Reprinted in *The Long View*.

Selected Bibliography

PRIMARY SOURCES

I. *Juvenilia: Contributions to* Natal University College Magazine
from 1920 to 1924

Poems: "To a Picture," signed UBI, III (November, 1920), 8; "The
Sea," signed L. T., IV (June, 1921), 48–49; "Ladysmith (Midnight on the Battlefields)," signed A. P., V (November, 1921),
10–11; "Sonnets," signed A. S. P., VI (June, 1922), 19–20; "Sonnet—To Sleep," signed O. F., p. 29, and "Song of the Northward-
Bound," signed A. S. P., pp. 34–35, VII (Winter Term, 1922);
"Old Till," signed A. S. P., p. 7; "House of Dreams," signed K. S.,
p. 15, and "To ———," signed N. B., pp. 88–89, IX (October,
1923); "Curlilocks, Curlilocks, will you be mine?" unsigned, p. 18,
"Sonnet," signed A. S. P., p. 26, "Gemellia," signed A. S. P., p.
26, and "Felip'," unsigned, pp. 38–40, X (June, 1924).

Prose: "On Boots" (prose fantasy), VI (June, 1922), 9–11; "The
Imperial Conference" (two letters from Alan Paton, representative to the Imperial Conference of Students in England), XI (October, 1924), 9–12.

Drama: "His Excellency the Governor" (Shakespearian blank verse.
A circular drama in three short acts), IX (October, 1923), 17–
22; "Minutes of any Meeting of the ——— Society," (one-act
sketch), IX (October, 1923), 63–66.

"The New Physics" (poem), *Natal University College Magazine,
Commemoration Number, 1909–34,* (1934), pp. 37–39.

II. *Early Writings on Social and Public Affairs*

"Jan Hendrik Hofmeyr: An Appreciation," *South African Opinion,*
(September 18, 1936), pp. 7, 12.

"New Schools for South Africans," *Mentor* (Organ of the Natal Teachers' Society), (June 1942), pp. 5–7.

Series of articles on society and the offender in *The Forum* (South
African fortnightly of liberal opinion): "Punishment and Crime:
False Reasoning in Society's Attitude Towards the Offender," VI,
No. 25 (September 18, 1943), 5, 6, and 34; "Society Aims to

Protect Itself: How Effective is Severity of Punishment as a De-
terrent Against Crime?", VI, No. 29 (October 16, 1943), 25–27;
"Significance of Social Disapproval," VI, No. 36 (December 4,
1943), 25–27; "Real Way to Cure Crime: Our Society Must Reform Itself," IV, No. 44 (January 29, 1944), 24–26; "A Plan for
Model Prisons," VI, No. 52 (March 25, 1944), 24–26; "Let's Build
Model Prisons: Enlightened Reform Would Result in a Vast Saving in Human Material," VII, No. 6 (May 27, 1944), 5, 6, and 24.

"Educational Needs of the Adolescent" (in two parts), *Transvaal
Education News,* XL (September, 1944), 13–15; and XL (October 1944), 6–9.

"The Prevention of Crime," *Race Relations: Special Crime Number,*
XII, Nos. 3 and 4 (1945), 69–77. (Address to a National Conference.)

The Non-European Offender (Penal Reform Series No. 2). Johannesburg: South African Institute of Race Relations, 1945, 12 pp. (An
address to the National Social Welfare Conference, September,
1944.)

"Who is Really to Blame for the Crime Wave in South Africa?", *The
Forum,* VIII, No. 37 (December 15, 1945), 7–8.

"Behandling van die Oortreder" (Afrikaans—translation: "Treatment
of Offenders"), *Nongquai* (official news magazine of the South
African Police Forces), XXXVII (July 1946), 34–35.

"Great Conference of Christians and Jews at Oxford," *Outspan* (pop-
ular South African weekly), XL (September 13, 1946), 34–35.

"Penal Practice of Some Other Countries" (in two parts), *Nongquai,*
XXXVIII (July 1947), 876–878; and XXXVIII (August 1947),
1013–17.

"Child in Trouble," *Mentor,* XXX, No. 7 (October 1948), 2–9.

Freedom as a Reformatory Instrument (Penal Reform Pamphlets No.
2). Pretoria: Penal Reform League of South Africa, 1948, 15 pp.

"Juvenile Delinquency and Its Treatment," *Community and Crime,
Number 2, 1948* (Penal Reform Pamphlets No. 3). Pretoria: Van
Schaik, 1949, pp. 52–62.

"A Step Forward," *Theoria,* IV (1952), 6–9. (Introductory remarks
opening a Conference on The Treatment of Offenders, Durban,
October, 1951.)

III. *Principal Works: Fiction, Drama, Biography, Non-Fiction,
and Poetry*

Cry, the Beloved Country. New York: Charles Scribner's Sons, 1948,
278 pp. Dedication: "To Aubrey and Marigold Burns of Fairfax,
California." Reissued: Scribner's *Modern Standard Authors,* with
Author's Note and an introduction by Lewis Gannett, 1950; re-

printed 1954; reprinted 1959, with Second Author's Note, p. x (October 27, 1959).

Cry, the Beloved Country: A Story of Comfort in Desolation. London: Jonathan Cape, 1948, 269 pp. Dedication: "To my wife and to my friend of many years Jan Hendrik Hofmeyr."

Cry, the Beloved Country, (Braille—3 volumes). Mt. Healthy, Ohio: Clovernook Printing House for the Blind, 1949.

Cry, the Beloved Country, adaptations: See notes 1, 2, and 3 to Chapter One.

Cry, the Beloved Country, translations: See note 4 to Chapter One.

Too Late the Phalarope. Cape Town: Cannon (for Jonathan Cape), 1953, 283 pp. Translated into most of the languages listed for *Cry, the Beloved Country,* note 4, Chapter One.

Too Late the Phalarope. New York: Charles Scribner's Sons, 1953, 283 pp.

Too Late the Phalarope, a drama by ROBERT YALE LIBOTT from the novel by ALAN PATON. Presented by Mark K. Frank and directed by John Stix at the Belasco Theater, New York, on October 11, 1965. Typescript available at the Research Library of the Performing Arts, New York Public Library at Lincoln Center.

Tales from a Troubled Land. New York: Charles Scribner's Sons, 1961, 128 pp. (Published in Great Britain as *Debbie Go Home.* See listing below.) Ten short stories. Seven previously published: "The Worst Thing of His Life," *Trek,* XV (November 1951), 3–4; "Death of a Tsotsi," *Trek,* XVI (March 1952), 6–7; "Ha' penny," *South African PEN Yearbook, 1955,* pp. 41–44; "The Waste Land," *South African PEN Yearbook, 1956–57,* pp. 52–54; "Debbie Go Home," *Africa South,* III, No. 3 (April–June 1959), 118–127; "A Drink in the Passage," *Africa South,* IV, No. 3 (April–June 1960), 117–123; "Sponono," *South African PEN Yearbook, 1960; Esquire,* IV (April 1961), 8–11. Three stories published for the first time: "Life for a Life," "The Elephant Shooter," and "The Divided House."

Debbie Go Home. London: Jonathan Cape, 1961, 127 pp. The same ten short stories as in *Tales from a Troubled Land,* differently arranged.

The Last Journey (drama). Not published, but produced by the Waddington Players (an amateur group) at Lusaka, Northern Rhodesia (Zambia), 1959.

Mkhumbane (Village in the Gulley). Libretto for a musical by TODD MATSHIKIZA performed in Durban City Hall, Durban, South Africa, on March 21–27, 1960. Not published or revived, because Todd Matshikiza's score has not been available. Typescript is in possession of Alan Paton.

Sponono (with KRISHNA SHAH). New York: Charles Scribner's Sons, 1965, 190 pp. A play in three acts, based on three stories by Alan Paton.

Hofmeyr. Capetown: Oxford University Press, 1964, 545 pp. (Published in the United States as *South African Tragedy: The Life and Times of Jan Hofmeyr*. See following listing.)

South African Tragedy: The Life and Times of Jan Hofmeyr. Abridgement by DUDLEY C. LUNT; Prefatory Note, vii-x; Editorial Note, p. 413–415. New York: Scribner's, 1965, 415 pp.

South Africa Today (Public Affairs Pamphlet No. 175). New York: Public Affairs Committee, 1951; London: Lutterworth Press, 1953, 32 pp.

Christian Unity: A South African View (Third Peter Ainslie Memorial Lecture). Grahamstown: Rhodes University Press, 1951, 12 pp.

Salute to My Greatgrandchildren. Johannesburg: St. Benedict's Press, 1954, 20 pp. (Cover label erroneously printed as *Salute to My Great-Great-Grandchildren*.) Letters addressed to the Twenty-First Century.

The Land and People of South Africa (Portraits of the Nations Series). Philadelphia: Lippincott, 1955, 143 pp. (Published in Britain as *South Africa and Her People*. London: Lutterworth, 1957.)

South Africa in Transition (with DAN WEINER). Text by ALAN PATON and photographs by DAN WEINER. New York: Charles Scribner's Sons, 1956, 84 pp.

The People Wept: Being a Brief Account of the Origin, Contents, and Application of that Unjust Law of the Union of South Africa Known as The Group Areas Act of 1950 (Since Consolidated as Act No. 77 of 1957). Kloof, Natal: Alan Paton, 1958, 44 pp.

Hope for South Africa. London: Pall Mall Press, 1958; New York: Praeger, 1959, 94 pp.

The Christian Approach to Racial Problems in the Modern World (A Christian Action Pamphlet). London: Christian Action, 1959, 13 pp.

The Charlestown Story. Pietermaritzburg: Liberal Party Publication, 1960, 26 pp. Pamphlet explaining the effects of the Group Areas Act on Africans removed from land in Charlestown.

The Long View, New York: Praeger, 1967. A collection of Paton's essays compiled by EDWARD CALLAN comprising the series, "The Long View," with an introduction by Alan Paton, his Freedom Award Speech (1960), and "A Deep Experience."

IV *Later Poetry and Uncollected Fiction*

Four Poems, "To a Small Boy Who Died at Diepkloof Reformatory,"
"Sanna," "The Discardment," and "Samuel," in GUY BUTLER (ed.),
A Book of South African Verse (Oxford University Press, 1959),
pp. 67–72; "To a Small Boy Who Died at Diepkloof Reforma-
tory," in ROY MACNAB (ed.), *Towards the Sun* (London: Collins,
1950); "Toll Iron Bell, Toll Extolling Bell . . ." *The Forum*
(February 26, 1949), in an article, "Why Did Jan Hofmeyr Not
Found a Liberal Party?", reprinted in *Hofmeyr* and *South African
Tragedy;* "Apartheid," in *Salute to My Greatgrandchildren* (Jo-
hannesburg, 1952), and also *South African Outlook*, LXXXIII
(January 1, 1953), 16 (reprinted from *The Star*, a Johannesburg
newspaper); "A Psalm (I have seen my Lord in the forest . . .),"
South African Outlook, LXXXIII (July 1, 1953), 110; "A Psalm
(My Lord has a great attraction for the humble and simple
. . .)," *South African Outlook*, LXXXIII (October 1, 1953), 148;
Meditation for a Young Boy Confirmed. London: Society for
Promoting Christian Knowledge, 1959, 15 pp. [reprinted from
Theology, LXI (August 1958); previously appeared in *The
Christian Century*, LXXI (October 13, 1954), 1237–39]; "My
Great Discovery," *Africa South*, I (April-June, 1957), 94–97; "To
a Person Who Fled to Rhodesia," *Contact*, I, No. 12 (July 12,
1958), 12; "I have Approached a Moment of Sterility," *Contrast*,
I, No. 4 (1961), 17; "Stevie," a sketch (uncollected fiction),
Southern Review (Natal), I, No. 6 (September-October 1952),
3–4.

V *Later Articles, Introductions to Books, and Interviews*

"Africa Reporting," *New York Times Book Review* (February 20,
1949), 5, 26.

"Why Did Jan Hofmeyr Not Found a Liberal Party?" *The Forum*
(February 26, 1949). Contains the poem, "Toll Iron Bell, Toll
Extolling Bell . . ."

"*Saturday Review* Anisfield-Wolf Awards," *Saturday Review*, XXXII
(May 21, 1949), 22. Letter from Alan Paton.

"Toward a Spiritual Community," *Christian Century*, LXVII (March
8, 1950), 298–300.

"Racial Situation in South Africa: A Struggle Between Justice and
Survival," *African World*, (April, 1950), 17–18.

Address to the Johannesburg Business and Professional Women's Club
on the occasion of United Nation's Day, 1950. Available in the
Library of the South African Institute of Race Relations.

"The Unrecognized Power," *Saturday Review*, XXXIV (November 25,

1951), 10–11, 38–40. (This essay is Paton's contribution to *Religious Faith and World Culture*. See following listing.)

"Religious Faith and Human Brotherhood," in *Religious Faith and World Culture*, ed. A. W. LOOS. New York: Prentice-Hall, 1951. (Also appeared in *Explorations*. See listing following.)

"Religious Faith and Human Brotherhood," in *Explorations*, ed. T. C. POLLOCK *et al.* Englewood Cliffs, New Jersey: Prentice-Hall, Inc., 1956, pp. 751–60.

"Christian Unity: A South African View" (Third Peter Ainslie Memorial Lecture, 1951), *South African Outlook*, LXXI (October, 1951), 148–52. (Published as a separate publication—Grahamstown: Rhodes University, 1951.)

"Force Won't Solve South Africa's Problems," *The Forum*, I, No. 1 (April 1952), 4–6.

"South Africa Today," a series of three articles in *Southern Review* (Natal, South Africa). (1) I, No. 1 (April 1952), 1–5; (2) I, No. 2 (May 1952), 1–4; (3) I, No. 3 (June 1952), 1–4.

"Africa, Wakening, Challenges the World," *New York Times Magazine* (July 6, 1952), 6, 25–26.

"The White Man's Dilemna," *Saturday Review*, XXVI (May 2, 1953), 12–13, 53–54.

"America and the Challenge of Africa," (with HAROLD ISAACS), *Saturday Review*, XXVI (May 2, 1953), 9.

"Impending Tragedy," *Life*, XXIV (May 4, 1953), 163–170. Also appeared in *Life* (International Edition), XIV, No. 12 (June 15, 1953), 77–80.

"Crisis of White Supremacy," *The Forum* (July, 1953), 2–3.

"Liberal Approach," *New York Times Magazine* (August 9, 1953), pp. 20–23. (South African Liberal Party's approach to race relations; an appendage to an article by Albion Ross.)

"Letter from Alan Paton," *Saturday Review*, XXVI (August 9, 1953), 10.

"The English Speaking Churches and the Colour Bar," *The Forum*, II, New Series, No. 7 (October 1953), 17–18. (Brief account of some contemporary events.)

"The Church Amid Racial Tensions," *Christian Century*, LXXI (March 31, 1954), 393–94. Reprinted in *The Christian Century Reader*, 1962.

"Negro in America Today," *Colliers*, CXXXIV (October 15, 1954), 20, 52–56. (On the Negro in the southern American states.)

"Negro in the North," *Colliers*, CXXXIV (October 29, 1954), 70–80.

"The Novelist and Christ," (with LISTON POPE), *Saturday Review*, XXVII (December 4, 1954), 15–16, 56–57. (Problems of Christ-symbols in the novel.)

"Time, Gentlemen, Time," *The Forum*, IV (February 1955).

"Grim Drama in Johannesburg," *New York Times Magazine* (February 27, 1955), 15, 36, 38, 40.

"Olive Schreiner—The Forerunner," *The Forum*, IV, No. 1 (April 1955), 25–29.

"African Advancement: A Problem of Both Copperbelt and Federation," *Optima*, V (December 1955), 105–109. Reprinted in *Rhodesian Mining Journal*, XVIII (January 1965), 11–14.

"School in Danger," *Christian Century*, LXXII (December 28, 1955), 1524–25.

"Tragedy of the Beloved Country," *Coronet* (May 5, 1956), 40, 64–69.

"The South African Novel in English," in *Report of a Conference of Writers, Publishers, Editors and University Teachers of English Held at the University of Witwatersrand, Johannesburg, July 10–12, 1956*. Johannesburg: Witwatersrand University Press, 1957, pp. 145–157.

"The Tragic and Lovely Land of South Africa," *Holiday* (February 1957), 34–42, 119–121.

"Civil Rights in a Multi-Racial Society" (paper read at a Conference held at Witwatersrand University, 1957). Available in the Library of the South African Institute of Race Relations.

"Association by Permission," *Africa South*, I (July–September 1957), 11–20. (An account of the Native Laws Amendment Bill [1957] which prevents inter-racial association.)

"On Trial for Treason," *New Republic*, CXXXVII (November 11, 1957), 9–12. (Report on the Preparatory Examination of the South African Treason Trial.)

"Roy Campbell: Poet and Man," *Theoria*, IX (1957), 19–31.

"The Person in Community," in *The Christian Idea of Education Papers and Discussion*, ed. EDMUND FULLER. New Haven: Yale University Press, 1957.

"Church, State and Race," a series of two articles appearing in *Christian Century*, LXXV. (1) (February 26, 1958), 248–249; (2) (March 5, 1958), 278–280.

"Kirche, Staat und Rasse (aus dem Englischen übersetzt)," *Zeitschrift für die Alttestamentliche Wissenschaft*, IV (January, 1960), 1–9.

"The Attitude of the Church and the Christian towards the State," *Background Information to Church and Society*, No. 19 (March, 1958).

"The Crusader on a Polo Pony," *Contact* (April 5, 1958). On Peter Brown, National Chairman of the Liberal Party.

Introduction to *Durban: A Study in Racial Ecology* by LEO KUPER, HILSTAN WATTS, and RONALD DAVIES. London: Jonathan Cape,

1958; New York: Columbia University Press, 1958, pp. 13–16.

"The Long View," a series written for the Liberal Party fortnightly, *Contact*. Appeared in three groups: (1) from February 8, 1958, to January 24, 1959; (2) from April 16, 1960, to August 27, 1960; (3) from January 24, 1964, to the present. (*Contact* began to appear monthly, and then infrequently.) Reprinted in *The Long View* (New York, 1967). For complete listing see *The Long View*.

The Days of White Supremacy Are Over (*Contact* Pamphlet No. 2). Capetown, 1959, 6 pp. Separate publication of the column ending the first series in *Contact*, II, No. 2 (January 24, 1959), 9.

"Some Thoughts on the Contemporary Novel in Afrikaans," *English Studies in Africa*, II (September 1959), 159–166.

"Letter from Alan Paton," *English Studies in Africa*, III (March 1960), 102. (Corrects inaccurately printed statement in September, 1959 issue to: "it would be difficult for a white writer to create a non-white character.")

"South Africa, 1959," *Christianity and Crisis*, XIX (May 11, 1959), 64–67.

"South African Treason Trial," *Atlantic*, CCV (January 1960), 78–81.

"As Blind as Samson Was," *New York Times Magazine*, (April 10, 1960), 9–11, 104–109. (Attempts to depict the white South African who unreservedly supports *apartheid*). Reprinted in *The New York Times Background and Foreground*, (1961), pp. 107–116.

"Address by Alan Paton Accepting the Freedom House Award, October 5, 1960." Excerpts in the *New Leader*, XLIII (November 14, 1960), 15; reprinted in *The Long View* (New York, 1967).

"White Dilemma in Black Africa," *New York Times Magazine* (September 4, 1960), 8, 30–31.

"The Road," *New Yorker*, XXVI (December 17, 1960), 32–33. (Account of interview with the *New Yorker* editors in "Talk of the Town.")

"Africa, Christianity and the West," *Christianity and Crisis*, XX (December 26, 1960), 195–198.

Introduction to *Brief Authority* by CHARLES HOOPER. London: Collins, 1960, pp. 15–19.

"Cottlesloe Consultation," *The Compass* (February 1961). A (participant's account of the Consultations convened by the World Council of Churches. The purpose was to bring together South African religious leaders of differing convictions to investigate the racial situation in their country.)

"Republic for which South Africa Stands," *New York Times Magazine*.

(May 28, 1961), 9, 42–43. (On South Africa's withdrawal from the Commonwealth.)

"A Deep Experience" (personal biography), *Contrast,* I, No. 4 (December 1961), 20–24.

"South Africa's Black Stallion," *Manchester Guardian Weekly* (January 25, 1962), p. 11. (Review of Albert Luthuli's *Let My People Go.*)

"Four Interviews in South Africa: Alan Paton," by STUDS TERKEL. *Perspective on Ideas and the Arts* (Radio Station WFMT, Chicago, publication), XII, No. 5 (May 1963), 24–29.

"The Abuse of Power" (Address by Alan Paton at the Public Opening of the National Congress of the Liberal Party at Cape Town in 1963), *Liberal Opinion,* II, No. 4 (September 1963), 5–9.

"Trevor Huddleston," in *Thirteen for Christ,* ed. MELVILLE HARCOURT. New York: Sheed and Ward, 1963.

"Our New Africa," *Maryknoll,* Volume 57 (November 1963), 9–13.

"Four Splendid Voices," an essay introducing a collection of short stories by Alex LaGuma, James Matthews, Alf Wannenburg, and Richard Rive in *Quartet: New Voices from South Africa,* ed. RICHARD RIVE. New York: Crown, 1963, pp. 11–14.

"The Hofmeyr Biography," *Contrast,* III (October 1964), 32–36.

"A Personal View" (a comment by the co-author on *Sponono*). *New York Times,* March 29, 1964, Section 2, p. 1, columns 1–2.

"Liberals Reject Violence" (Address by the National President, Mr. Alan Paton, at the Liberal Party National Conference in Johannesburg on October 9 and 10, 1964). *Liberal Opinion,* III, No. 4 (October 1964), 1–4.

"A Special Report on the Republic of South Africa, 1965" (illustrated), *Presbyterian Life,* XVIII, No. 11 (June 1, 1965), 6–11. The same article appears simultaneously in *The Lutheran, The Episcopalian,* and *Commonweal,* LXXXII (May 28, 1965), 311–315.

"Beware of Melancholy," *Christianity and Crisis,* XXV (November 1, 1965), 223–24. Reprinted from Paton's column "The Long View," *Contact,* VIII, No. 7 (July 1965), 2–3.

SECONDARY SOURCES

There are at present no books on Alan Paton. The following are among the more useful articles in books and periodicals.

BREIT, HARVEY. *The Writer Observed.* New York: World, 1956. Contains an interview with Alan Paton.

DAVIES, HORTON. *A Mirror For the Ministry in Modern Novels.* New

York: Oxford University Press, 1959. Gives an analysis of *Cry, the Beloved Country*.

————. "Alan Paton: Literary Artist and Anglican," *The Hibbert Journal*, I (April, 1952), 262–268. Contains valuable biographical material.

DRIVER, JONTY. "Alan Paton's *Hofmeyr*," *Race*, IV (April 1965), 269–280. A review article.

FULLER, EDMUND. "Alan Paton: Tragedy and Beyond," in *Books with the Man Behind Them*. New York: Random House, 1962, pp. 83–101. A perceptive account of the literary qualities of Paton's novels.

GARDINER, HAROLD. *In All Conscience: Reflections on Books and Culture*. New York: Hanover House, 1959. Reprints Gardiner's reviews in America of *Cry, the Beloved Country* and *Too Late the Phalarope*, pp. 108–116.

GASSNER, JOHN. *Theatre at the Crossroads*. New York: Holt, 1960. Discusses R. L. Libott's dramatization of *Cry, the Beloved Country*.

HUDDLESTON, TREVOR. *Naught for Your Comfort*. New York: Doubleday, 1956. Valuable for background information.

PRESCOTT, ORVILLE. *In My Opinion: An Inquiry Into the Contemporary Novel*. New York: Bobbs-Merrill, 1952. Selects *Cry, the Beloved Country* as one of the four great novels of recent years.

MARQUARD, LEO. *The Peoples and Policies of South Africa*. New York: Oxford University Press, 1960. Historical background by a leader of the Liberal Party and noted historian.

ROONEY, CHARLES. "The 'Message' of Alan Paton," *Catholic World* (November 1961), pp. 92–98. An analysis of Paton's fiction including the short stories in *Tales From a Troubled Land*.

WORSLEY, T. C. "A Modern Morality," *New Statesman and Nation*, XLVII (February 6, 1964), 159. On Felicia Komai's dramatizaton of *Cry, the Beloved Country*.

Index